THE EMPOWERED MIND

How to Harness the Creative Force Within You

Gini Graham Scott
Ph.D, J.D.

PRENTICE HALL
Englewood Cliffs, New Jersey 07632

Prentice-Hall International (UK) Limited, *London*
Prentice-Hall of Australia Pty. Limited, *Sydney*
Prentice-Hall Canada, Inc., *Toronto*
Prentice-Hall Hispanoamericana, S.A., *Mexico*
Prentice-Hall of India Private Limited, *New Delhi*
Prentice-Hall of Japan, Inc., *Tokyo*
Simon & Schuster Asia Pte. Ltd., *Singapore*
Editora Prentice-Hall do Brasil, Ltda., *Rio de Janeiro*

© 1994 *by*

Prentice Hall
Englewood Cliffs, New Jersey

10 9 8 7 6 5 4 3 2

Library of Congress Cataloging in Publication Data

Scott, Gini Graham.
   The empowered mind : how to harness the creative force within you
/ Gini Graham Scott.
     p. cm.
   Includes index.
   ISBN 0-13-143868-9. — ISBN 0-13-143876-X
   1. Success—Psychological aspects. I. Title.
BF637.S8S386   1994
158—dc20
                                            93-30518
                                              CIP

ISBN 0-13-143868-9

ISBN 0-13-143876-X (paper)

PRENTICE HALL
Career & Personal Development
Englewood Cliffs, NJ 07632

Simon & Schuster, A Paramount Communications Company

Printed in the United States of America

INTRODUCTION
Discover Your Creative Force

*T*he powerful "creative force" techniques described in this book are designed to help you discover the inner powers of your mind and use them to empower yourself to get what you want—and to feel more satisfaction—at work and in your personal life. In today's competitive global economy, most of us are concerned about doing the best we can at work to gain that competitive edge. We want to achieve excellence in performance and service. And we want the satisfaction that comes from achieving our personal goals.

Both are possible. You can enjoy being and doing your best; you can achieve your business and personal goals, and you can have fun and satisfaction along with success. There's no need to be stressed out about doing well and being the best you can be.

Everyone can do this, because everyone has these "creative force" abilities. However, many people don't use or fully develop them. *The Empowered Mind* will show you how to tap these powers, so you can have both—success and satisfaction—and the inner sense of security, and the self-esteem that comes from finding your purpose in this time of rapid and confusing social change.

∎What the Creative Force Techniques Did for Me

I wrote this book after working with and refining these techniques for over twenty years, by using them continually in my work and in everyday situations. For example, I used them to write more than twenty published books in ten years; to get more than two dozen games on the market with different game companies; and to design several lines of dolls and fantasy creatures, write children's books, and take photographs that have been published in a book and calendar. In addition, without formal training in the field, I was able to set up a PR program, an organizational development program, and a management training program for an organization with more than 350 members by tapping into these inner creative powers to sense what the organization needed and how to fill those needs (I later wrote two books showing others how to do similar things).

Then, too, I have used these techniques to do things I once thought I never could do, including becoming a speaker and a workshop/seminar leader (I used to be terrified of public speaking); writing country and pop songs, some of which have been published and recorded (I used to think I couldn't carry a tune); and becoming a marketing and sales trainer and consultant (I used to hate selling and was not very persuasive). I also drew on these techniques to get through law school in four and a half years, while working almost full time as a writer (at one time, I was terrified of taking tests and did not think myself smart enough to do any of this).

Plus, I have used these techniques to make business decisions to select people with whom to work, to choose projects on which to work, and to sense unanticipated opportunities that led to successful ventures. I bring up these experiences not to brag, but to illustrate what is possible when we tap into this inner creative part of ourselves and direct it to help us achieve the goals and make the world we want.

Since these techniques have worked so well for me, I want to share them with you. I originally wrote about some of them in my book *Mind Power: Picture Your Way to Success in Business*. Now, after additional work with these techniques, I have further developed and refined them. *The Empowered Mind* represents a culmination of these efforts and expands on what has gone before.

■What Creative Force Techniques Will Do for You

You'll find these techniques will help you to:

➤ feel more powerful, and as you get in touch with your own power, to be able to do more of what you want to do;

➤ gain more confidence and self-esteem as you discover yourself getting the results you want;

➤ develop a greater sense of personal identity and purpose as you clarify your direction and goals and find everything working better in your life;

➤ be more satisfied with what you are doing and who you are;

➤ get more enjoyment out of everyday life—including ordinary, routine activities and experiences that might otherwise cause upset and stress.

How? By harnessing the creative force within, you will be able to:

Focus Your Energy for Optimum Functioning. In today's fast-paced and ever-changing world, it's crucial to be adaptable and flexible and to keep a balance so you can react appropriately. This way you can speed up and slow down when you want to; raise your energy or relax as you need to; and discover that happy mean between enjoyable stimulation and enervating, destructive stress. For example, after a tense day at work, you'll be able to wind down quickly and relax; on the other hand, if you have an important presentation to make but feel tired or not in the mood, you'll be able to harness that extra boost of energy and enthusiasm you need to get results.

Maximize Your Talents. When you do your best at something, you not only feel a sense of accomplishment, but you experience the thrill that comes from being recognized by others for it. And this recognition may not only open doors to a desirable career, it may help you feel a sense of having achieved your purpose in life—a very powerful feeling. In turn, these creative force techniques can help you discover your deeper mission and abilities and energize you to develop them to the fullest.

Design the Person You Want to Be. Who would you like to be? Who are your role models? How would you like to change? Do you need to create a different image for yourself in order to step into a new job you want? To achieve a desired goal, you may need to make some changes in your personal style, in your personality, or in your appearance. Perhaps you want to work for a particular company or to change careers. If so, you may need to change the way you present yourself to fit into the culture of that company or field. With these creative force techniques, you'll discover how you need to change and then put your discoveries into practice.

Become Smarter by Sharpening Your Intellectual Powers. In today's information age, people need to be smarter than ever. The empowered-mind techniques will help you to boost your inner mental powers; to sharpen your thinking and your ability to learn, know, and remember more; and to absorb the new information you need to move ahead. They will also help you to be a brighter, wittier, more interesting companion, which can help you in your personal relationships with partners and friends.

Increase Your Powers of Perception and Awareness. If we only pay attention, we can perceive and be aware of so much more. For example, when should you trust someone; what are the warning signs that a person isn't being honest with you? Is the message you are trying to convey getting through, or are there cues that signal the opposite—that the person really isn't interested or that you are presenting the message in the wrong way? Is there danger ahead? Can you take steps to avoid the problem? Do colleagues have a hidden agenda that you need to discover in order to avoid a serious confrontation or to avoid having your plans sabotaged? The empowered mind techniques can help you zero in on just what is going on so you can act appropriately.

Make Better Decisions. Today, we have many options: choices about careers, about recreation, about lifestyles, about new business opportunities, and more. There are so many possibilities, and frequently we have to decide what to do quickly, intuitively. If we are in touch with the inner cues that give us insights and suggestions, we can make much better choices. Tapping into your inner creative force can help you choose.

Turn Your Problems into Possibilities. The flip side of every problem is a possibility. Part of that transformation comes from seeing each problem as a stepping-stone or a learning experience. By tapping into your inner powers, you can imagine alternatives and options and can make other intuitive leaps that will enable you to achieve truly creative positive gains. For example, a lost job may be a chance to discover new talents and business leadership abilities; a break-up with a long-term partner may be a chance to express new creative parts of your personality so you can find an even more satisfying relationship; a conflict with a difficult person at work may help you to develop new styles for conflict resolution that you can transfer into other settings. These empowered-mind techniques will help you to creatively imagine these possibilities and put them into action.

Optimize Your Relationships. The key to better relationships is understanding others and improving your ability to communicate with them. So many relationships founder on a lack of insight or on communication breakdowns. Also, improved understanding and communication can help you to recognize what others need and want, so you can provide it and can motivate them to act. Creative-force techniques will help you tap into what to say and do and will then help you put this knowledge into practice. The benefits are unlimited: more personal satisfaction, a more supportive working environment, career advancement, more of whatever you want.

■How to Use this Book

And these are just some of the benefits you'll gain.

Use this book to learn how to tap into the creative force within, discover how to call on it in any situation. Use it to learn specific techniques you can apply in particular situations. These techniques are tools designed to help you tap that force; once you do, you can adapt the exercises or create your own ways to unleash these abilities. The exercises I have suggested are ones that have worked for me and others. The examples presented show how different people used these techniques in different situations. Their experiences may suggest other possible uses. But the power of the creative force is such that once you understand the basic principles, you can use these tools to create your own techniques and tools and make these methods your own. You can build on and further develop your abilities. It's like tapping into a universal source of energy within you—and once you do, you can use the techniques to direct that energy to help you determine, prioritize, and achieve your goals.

Here are some ways you can get the most from this book:

➤ Read the first three chapters for an overview of what the creative force is, how you can access it, why these techniques work, and how to maximize the effects of the very important tool of brainstorming.

➤ Think about what you would most like to gain from using these techniques (for example, having more energy, increasing your creative potential, setting and achieving goals, problem-solving or decision-making, improving a relationship) and look in the table of contents for the chapter that deals with this topic.

➤ Then, turn to that chapter and use the exercises to focus on your priorities. Select those exercises that you feel are most applicable to your particular situation. Approximate times listed for each exercise are intended purely as guidelines. You may find you can do these much more quickly or may prefer to spend more time than suggested.

➤ Use the charts and forms that accompany many of the exercises to record your insights and ideas—either during or after the exercise. They will help you focus on your choices and alternatives and lead you to the next step.

➤ Try to spend about ten to twenty minutes a day working with these techniques. Make them a familiar, comfortable part of your everyday life. Regular practice will help you keep your empowered mind techniques really sharp.

➤ Keep a record of what you do. Save the charts and forms you fill out and record any subsequent reflections that may result from using these techniques. Review them every so often to see what you have accomplished.

But, most important, with the empowered mind techniques you are really learning a way of life—a new way to view your experiences—a way that will help you become more aware, perceptive, and better able to respond appropriately in any situation. As a result you'll be able to do what's best for you, because you will be acting from that deeper intuitive knowing and inner energy that flows from your creative force.

TABLE OF CONTENTS

CHAPTER 18:
■Orchestrate Your Thinking: Make Everyday Experiences
Exciting and Productive *263*

CHAPTER 1

THE EMPOWERED MIND
Your Inner Radar
at Work

Judy, a researcher and writer, was working on a project with a partner who was supplying her with information based on his personal experience. As they worked together, Judy began to sense that her partner's anger over what had happened to him blurred his objectivity and that the information he was providing was less than accurate. For awhile, she put her concerns aside; her partner kept assuring her that his anger was justified and that he was telling her the real inside truth. So she continued on, pushing her inner misgivings aside, since on the surface everything seemed fine.

But then, she received a warning letter about her partner from a lawyer representing one of the people about whom her partner was writing. This wasn't just a routine back-off letter from a lawyer, and she confronted her partner with it. His response was so irrational that she realized her inner warning signals were correct. In the past, she had sensed her partner's deep anger, but she had brushed these feelings aside. Now she broke off the original relationship, and once she did, she found herself attuned and

1

receptive to new possibilities that would make the project work without her partner.

In short, what Judy did was to tap into and listen to those inner sources of information that can be accessed only if we pay attention. They give us insights because on an intuitive or subconscious level we pick up a great deal of information about feelings, sensations, emotions, motivations, and beliefs about ourselves and others of which we are not otherwise aware. Similarly, these insights increase our chances of making correct predictions and making good choices. When we tune into this inner knowledge, we access a kind of inner radar that makes us more aware of the people and things around us and helps us achieve our objectives. Of course, we then have to act on this knowledge.

■Tune into Your Inner Radar

To use this inner knowledge, however, you first have to pay attention and notice it. It must be cultivated, or like an unnourished plant, it will start to wither and die (although, with the right attention, there is always the potential for revival).

Once you start noticing and developing this source of information and once you start recognizing when it is accurate and when to act on it, it is an extremely valuable tool. It can help you determine whether or not to trust or work with someone; whether or not to enter into a particular deal; whether to take one job or another. Listen to it and respond correctly, and you help to create better work opportunities, better personal relationships, better chances in whatever you do in life. But fail to listen to or pick up the wrong message, and the chances are you won't succeed.

Often we discount this ability, because in today's society we value being rational and making decisions in a reasoned, logical way. So in business we use management by objectives, path analysis, total quality control, and other techniques based on logical, linear thinking.

Such approaches are fine, of course, but we can also tap into our intuitive, nonrational side to gain insights and understandings that, when combined with rational techniques or used alone, can help us make even better decisions and choices.

This intuitive, nonrational side operates in two modes, and it is important to learn how to use both of them.

1. A *receptive mode*, which helps you tune into that inner knowledge and understanding, that you don't pick up rationally.

2. An *active mode*, which allows you to put into action the insights you have gained from that information. In particular, you can use this power to shape yourself, influence others, and affect events.

■How Your Empowered Mind Works

How do we get such insights? And why do they work? Researchers involved with brain research have been finding physical evidence for this power of the mind as they have been mapping the different parts of the brain. It is now widely agreed that the intuitive functions are associated with the operations of the right hemisphere of the brain, which perceives information in a holistic way: information comes in pictures, symbols, and metaphors. The analytical functions are associated with the operations of the left hemisphere of the brain, which perceives information in a logical, linear way, sequentially processing one bit of information at a time. It is, to quote Leonard Shlain, author of *Art and Physics*, the difference between the artist who sees in pictures and the physicist who analyzes in mathematical equations. Both may be seeing the same thing, but interpreting it differently—one in the language of symbol and metaphor, the other in the language of math.[1]

Essentially, what we are doing through these creative-force techniques is getting more in touch with this intuitive, creative part of ourselves so that we can see these pictures and perceive these feelings and sensations even before we are consciously aware of them. Becoming conscious or thinking about these things requires an additional step of transferring these pictures and images into our left brain for processing and analysis. But this thinking

---

1 Radio interview with Leonard Shlain, author of *Art and Physics* (William Morrow, 1991) on my program, *Changemakers*.

process takes time, delaying our insights. We can even distort these pictures by interpreting them incorrectly, explaining them away, or censoring them if they don't agree with what we would like to believe. When we learn to perceive this creative force directly, however, it can be a source of great information and energy.

We can learn to facilitate our own creative processes. Researchers have discovered that a variety of conditions contribute to the faster passage of thoughts through the brain. Our thoughts, they say, are like electrical currents, passing from cell to cell in the brain, traveling through a kind of chemical bath as they go. There are even electrode devices that enable you to see your own brain waves created as you think and image things, and if you are able to control your thinking and imaging processes, you can see your own brain waves change. Thus, if we can improve the chemical reactions or increase or facilitate the connections between nerves in the brain, we can speed our thoughts along. One way to do this is by chemical or electrical means, so-called "smart drugs" or "brain stimulators."[2] Another way is by using our powers of visualization and thought.

While much of this research has been directed toward showing how various chemical substances, such as those in the new generation of smart drugs and nutrients can increase mental functioning like memory and learning abilities, the research also suggests that mental activities might contribute to this improved biochemical state. Relaxation and meditation techniques have been shown to change brain waves, altering the underlying biochemistry that contributes to shaping these waves. In turn, the intuitive leaps and insights that may occur when a person is in an altered, more intuitive state of mind, may arise from this improved biochemical state.

Such research is in its early stages, but it appears that these underlying biochemical or electrical factors in the brain contribute to intuitive insights. At the same time, intuitive thinking itself may contribute to creating biochemical or electrical changes in the brain leading to still more insights. The process seems to occur

---

2 Ross Pelton, *Mind Food & Smart Pills*, New York: Doubleday, 1989, pp. 23–44.

in much the same way as the brainstorming process triggers still more ideas and creative leaps.

In short, by changing our own brain's biochemistry and electrical functioning with our thoughts, we unleash our creative forces.

■Getting the Most from the Empowered-Mind Techniques

Here are just some of the ways you can use these techniques. You will certainly think of others.

In the chart on page 6, you'll see a list of general benefits; next to each is an example of a specific application. On the line below the specific application listed, write down how you might apply that particular benefit to your own situation or need.

Another way to use this chart is to think of a specific result you want. Then think of the general things you will need to do or change about yourself to get that benefit. Say, for example, you want to create a new career for yourself in a different field. You might want to do the following:

➤ have more energy, so you can do the work you are doing now for income while you develop that new career;

➤ increase your feelings of confidence, so you can convince people in this new field you can do the job;

➤ overcome uncertainty, so you are really sure this is what you want to do;

➤ improve and perfect your talents, so you can effectively do the tasks required in this new situation;

➤ reshape your personality in a way that better suits your new job.

In short, as you empower yourself through tapping your inner creativity, you will find not only many *specific* ways to apply the general benefits you gain from these techniques, but you will be able to set specific goals to achieve and work backwards from them to determine what you need to do to reach that goal.

HOW THE EMPOWERED MIND TECHNIQUES CAN HELP YOU

General Benefits	*Examples of Specific Applications*
Overcome stress and relax	Get through a series of deadlines
Have more energy; overcome fatigue	Be alert at an important meeting
Feel more confident; have more self-esteem	Make a good impression at an interview
Overcome negative behavior patterns and blocks	Change behavior making another angry
Overcome uncertainty; decide what to do	Get over fear of making wrong choice
Recognize the possibilities	Break a log-jam with other alternatives
Discover a new direction for yourself	Choose the right new career path
Make the best decision	Decide whether to make a move or not
Set goals and determine the best steps to achieve them	Plan the steps for selling a new product

continued . . .

Turn around a difficult situation	Change an enemy into a friend
Improve and perfect your talents	Become a successful speaker
Become more creative and innovative	Come up with ideas for a PR campaign
Shape your desired personality/self-image	Become more outgoing to get a job
Become the best of who you are	Become an even better salesperson
Better understand others for better relationships	Recognize what someone *really* likes and doesn't like to get along better
Sense whether to trust others or not	Decide if the business deal is for real
Recognize the cues that motivate others	Find ways to make your boss say yes
Discover the solutions to problems	Discover how to make more money
Find ways to profit from your problems	See a money-making idea in a problem

How John J. Used the Power of Intuition to Start a Business

John J. had recently lost his business and was trying to decide what to do next. At his wife's insistence, he had gone to a self-help organization designed to assist people find jobs by holding work-shops, providing leads, and offering other programs. But he wasn't sure the group could really help him. As he sat there going through the introductory workshops dealing with how to assess job skills, write resumes, and conduct successful interviews, he wondered how all this really applied to him. He saw himself as an entre-preneur and really didn't want another job. What he wanted was to get his business—or maybe another business—going again.

So why was he here? He was about to walk out after the last workshop and tell his wife that, as promised, he had at least gone to the group's meetings, when suddenly he had a flash of insight. It was like a voice within him telling him to stay, that he could in fact use the group not to get a job, but to develop other skills and make contacts that he could then use to create another business. He wasn't sure exactly where that voice came from, but he felt this intense burst of energy that told him to listen to it. He decided to stay.

Basically, he sensed his creative force. Had he tried to analyze this sensation logically, it would have made no sense; in addition, it contradicted his earlier emotional response to resist getting in-volved. But the message from his deeper intuitive self was telling him to stay. It was giving him pictures of what staying might mean, what he could do with the group. All these intuitive insights came to him in a flash. If he hadn't been aware of this creative force within, he could easily have missed the signal, or he could easily have ignored or overridden the signal. But instead he felt its importance and power and decided to listen to it and follow it. With the empowered-mind techniques, you can learn to do this, too.

As a result, John worked with the group, which had a number of different departments (such as training and development, coun-seling, placement, and programming) that helped members with the job-seeking process. He joined one of these groups, began to move into management, and then set up several other departments in the organization. Based on the management and program-de-velopment skills he developed in working with this organization and the contacts he made through it, he was able to create a new business that marketed these skills to other companies.

As John's example illustrates, it is important to do four things in order to make use of this inner creative force:

1. Know that it is within you and that you can use it to guide you.

2. Pay attention when you feel this sense of energy rising within you (in whatever form it comes to you—as a voice, in pictures, or in feelings and sensations).

3. Notice what this energy is urging you to do.

4. Respond according to the way you feel this energy directing you.

The Danger of Not Listening to Your Creative Force

This intuitive energy is not only a signal to do something, it can be a warning not to do something. Henrietta's experience provides an example of what can occur when signals are ignored.

It was about 8:30 one fall evening and Henrietta was just leaving an art opening going to her car a few blocks away. It was a drizzly night, so there weren't many people on the dark downtown streets. When she saw what looked like four kids turn onto the street on the far corner about 100 feet away, a warning signal, like a bell or sudden tingling sensation, urged her to be cautious. For a moment, she was tempted to walk on the other side of the street. Then she heard what sounded like a more logical, reassuring voice override this signal, saying something like: . . . but they're just kids . . . it's early . . . there are other people out . . . don't act as if you're afraid by crossing the street . . . and if you just keep walking with confidence, as if you're not afraid, nothing will happen. The thoughts came quickly, and she kept going. After she passed the first pair of kids, she thought everything was fine, but then, just as she passed the second pair, an arm reached out, knocked her down, and grabbed her purse.

Fortunately, Henrietta wasn't hurt. But the experience taught her the importance of paying attention and listening to that inner signal and responding accordingly. Under other circumstances, Henrietta might have ignored such a signal and nothing might have happened; or even if she had responded and crossed the street, the kids might have still attacked.

What Henrietta's story illustrates is that your inner force can act like a kind of early warning signal. Responding to it can increase your chances of a favorable outcome; not responding can increase the chances of running into problems. As you learn to get in touch with this inner force, be sure to:

1. Listen to what it is telling you to do; and
2. Don't let your inner editor push this signal aside. If you get a strong clear signal, listen to it and act accordingly.

How Delores Used Intuition to Detect a Fraud

Your intuition can also be a powerful guide telling you when to trust and when not to. Delores discovered this when she relied on this inner signal to detect a fraud. She was working as a sales representative and hoping to start her own business when a good friend told her about a new program that she and about 10,000 other people nationally had joined. The program was unique. It involved putting up a few hundred dollars to participate in an unusual charitable trust. Delores' friend described the program as one headed by a sincere philanthropist, and Delores knew several other people who had become involved. But the whole arrangement sounded very strange—in the end the participants were supposed to receive many times that amount, depending upon how much they had invested. None of the people involved really understood much about the legal and financial ins and outs of how this trust worked, but everyone sincerely believed that this program was real and had complete faith in the leaders.

So should Delores join in? Her friend sent her some information showing the glowing credentials of the participants. And Delores knew some of the most influential people in her area were joining. But as she read the documents, she suddenly got the strong sense that this arrangement was not what it seemed. Despite the trappings that had persuaded so many thousands of people to believe in the program and the founders, she felt sure the project was a scam.

She had a sudden image of the pieces of a puzzle not fitting. There was a missing piece, and two other pieces overlapped. She realized that her intuition was trying to communicate with her. The picture of the puzzle seemed so clear and vivid that she felt the image had to be true.

Yet, was it? To check her insight, as well as to show goodwill to her friend, with whom she had worked on several business projects, she decided to join but to keep her investment down to the lowest possible amount. If she was wrong, she would reap some reward; and if she was right, she would be able to, at relatively little cost, test and further develop her ability to correctly sense and know things.

As it turned out, the warning message from her intuition was right on. Over the next few months, the payoff date was continually put off, and no one ever did receive anything. Delores' intuition had been like an inner radar, pointing up the underlying dishonesty of the key people involved. Then, trusting the strong picture she received, Delores was able knowingly to decide what to do. She could do this because she:

➤ knew the way in which her intuition communicated with her—through strong pictures that suddenly appeared in her mind's eye;

➤ was able to quickly interpret the meaning or message of these pictures.

■Accessing the Power of Your Intuition

As these stories illustrate, your mind's intuitive abilities can be a powerful tool if you develop and pay attention to them. Once you are able to tap into them, they are like a beacon lighting the way to a clear path ahead or pointing out the dangers along the way—signaling where to go, what problems to avoid, or what to do to prepare to successfully cope with and overcome the difficulties in your path. As you learn how to access this part of your mind, using the creative-force techniques described in this book, you will find countless ways to draw on these enhanced powers and apply them to all aspects of your life.

Using Visualization and Self-Hypnosis to Harness Your Intuition

I have been developing and using these techniques, which I first described in *Mind Power: Picture Your Way to Success,* for more than twenty years. They have become such an automatic part of my life that I just use them without thinking much about them. In turn, in the five years since writing *Mind Power,* I have received even further confirmation of the success of these techniques both in my own life and in the new research coming out about the new techniques to enhance brain functioning.

We are no longer necessarily limited by traditional barriers, such as having to acquire information through a step-by-step acquisition of knowledge. Instead, in many situations, we can learn in more global and graphic ways by using our inner abilities to imagine, visualize, experience, or sense how things go together. It's a kind of systems approach to learning and understanding where we can come to gain knowledge in a different way. Remember the earlier example of the artist and the mathematician? The artist sees things through image, symbol, and metaphor; the mathematician perceives through sequential building blocks of knowledge. The knowledge gained may be the same but the artist gains it differently and more completely. In his work on these two modes of perception, *Art and Physics,* Dr. Leonard Shlain suggests that the revolutionary artists who have changed our way of seeing the world have always intuitively known things before the physicists have; they have been like clairvoyants of the new paradigms of seeing reality, because they have seen in this more metaphorical, intuitive way.[3]

Similarly, if we can learn to tap into these intuitive powers and see in a global way, we have the ability to learn and understand things much more quickly. And we can use this greater awareness to know what to do now and how to get where we want to go next, for we can better view the past, envision the present, and prevision the future with these techniques.

---

[3] Radio interview with and lecture by Leonard Shlain, based on his book *Art and Physics.*

I first started using these creative visioning techniques in 1968 when I began designing games. This exploration began when I organized a games group. I started it since I loved playing games as a kid, and as a result of spending so much time launching the group and thinking about games, I began having occasional dreams about games. A friend suggested hypnosis to encourage me to come up with even more ideas, rather than waiting for random dreams, and he led me on my first guided journey into the intuitive part of my mind.

In the beginning, I needed the formal technique of going into an altered hypnotic state, at first with him guiding me and then by doing it myself. After awhile, I no longer needed any preparatory techniques, and, in an instant, I could imagine pictures of games and people playing them. Soon I found I could apply this technique of accessing my intuition to other creative projects. After awhile, I found I could apply it not only to specific projects but to making decisions and choices in my life generally. For example, I used it to help me imagine what I wanted to do next (try teaching at college for awhile) and where I wanted to teach (in the South for a different experience), and then I even imagined exactly the type of school I wanted it to be and what to say to get the job (which led to a six-months assistant professorship at a small university on the outskirts of Atlanta).

This intuitive technique was like having a magic genie I could call forth whenever I wanted help with things I wasn't finding the answers for using my logic. It was wonderful when I needed immediate answers to something, when I had to make a quick decision and didn't have the time to work the answer out logically. My intuition gave me quick insight enabling me to act—and almost always, the answer was not only quick, but right!

I supplemented my own explorations with these techniques by attending dozens of workshops on developing creativity, working with hypnosis, using visualization and imagery, meditating, and the like—all designed to expand the power of the mind. I kept testing what I learned in my own life through my own experiences, and I kept further refining these techniques.

The techniques described here represent the culmination of my work with these methods. I have found them effective in tapping the inner creative potential of my mind. You can use these same methods or feel free to adapt them by changing any imagery to suit your own style. For example, use a computer screen instead of a movie screen to see mental images, or, if you prefer, get this information in the form of voices or feelings, or imagine that you are getting information from a professor, CEO, counselor, or spiritual teacher instead of listening to an inner voice or guide.

The key to success is learning to adapt these basic procedures and techniques so they work for you. They will help you become:

➤ more *receptive* to notice the inner creative power within you, however it communicates with you—through seeing, hearing, feeling, or knowing—or a combination of these;

➤ *clearer* about your response to the knowledge you have gained;

➤ able to draw on your inner powers to *take action* to achieve your desired goals or avoid any difficulties or barriers you have perceived.

CHAPTER 2

HARNESS YOUR INTUITION

How to Know
When You Know

One of the most difficult things about using your intuition either to gain insights or to make choices is determining how you know your intuition is correct. How do you know when you know when you are working with something as subjective as intuition? In business, science, and the professions today, people use a variety of systems to make planning, setting strategies, and decision making as objective as possible. But in working with intuitive, gut-level sources of information and knowing, those systems don't work.

Nevertheless, you can still get a strong sense of whether your information or choice is right by measuring your *impression* of the intensity of your belief and your *sense* of the probabilities of being correct. For example, ask yourself, on a scale ranging from 0 to 100, how strongly do I believe what I believe, and see what number immediately flashes into your mind. Or ask yourself, on a scale of 0 to 100, how probable is it that the choice I am making is the right one and see what number comes to mind. If your response is high, say 70 or better, you probably feel very strongly that what you believe is true or that you are making the right decision; and if it's 90 or above, that's an even stronger indication that you feel certain about what you are doing. If you get a medium or weak response, you should reevaluate your belief or decision. You aren't really sure.

Although you are still measuring something subjective—your *impression* of the intensity of your belief; your *sense* of the probabilities—you are adding a second level of review that puts a little distance between you and your initial response. It's a way of double-checking or reconfirming your experience.

Another way to increase your confidence in your intuition is by testing the strength of your belief or the certainty of your decision in other situations. How likely are you to be correct when you have a strong belief or sense of making the right decision? (Use the form on page 17 to monitor how well your intuition worked.) Another way to test your intuition: When it turns out you were right about something, reflect back on how you felt when you believed something strongly or felt certain you were right. (Use the form on page 18 to monitor the results). Monitoring your feelings will help you evaluate all your intuitions, because you will experience similar sensations whenever you are correct. While not absolutely foolproof—it is, after all, based on subjective feelings, impressions, and beliefs—you can increase your chances for being correct or making the right choice by recognizing the signals.

■Learning to Trust Your Intuitive Power

Often you get feelings and premonitions that something will happen, and it turns out you are wrong. The outcome isn't as you believe or suspect it will be: Someone doesn't respond as you anticipated. Predicted dangers don't materialize. An expected event doesn't happen. Yet at other times, you are correct.

How can you know when you know? How can you measure the intensity of your belief and increase your chances of correctly interpreting your intuition? What, for example, would you have done in this situation?

When Julie's landlord raised her rent, she felt this was a signal to move. She had been feeling her apartment was too small.

TEST YOUR INTUITION 1: STRENGTH OF BELIEF

Belief that Something Will Happen	Strength of Belief (Scale 0–100)	Did It Happen? Yes No Unsure

TEST YOUR INTUITION 1: STRENGTH OF BELIEF

Difficult Decision	Strength of Belief (Scale 0–100)	Was Decision Correct: Yes No Unsure

TEST YOUR INTUITION 2: FEELING

Events about Which I Was Right	How I Felt When I Came to that Belief or Made that Decision (list sensations, impressions, images, etc.)

But, where? Should she stay in San Francisco or move to another city? She felt restless and was drawn to L.A.; it offered more opportunities. But should she pull up her roots?

About a week later, she went on a retreat, and, in an exercise, she saw herself living in a house on a hill by the ocean—it wasn't clear where it was.

She returned from the retreat more determined to move, but still debating where to go. To help her decide, she drove to a residential area near the ocean. She would want to live here if she stayed in San Francisco. She drove around looking for "For Rent" signs and imagining what it would be like to live there. Suddenly, she saw a house that looked perfect. It was just two blocks from the ocean and was shaded with trees. Though she couldn't see inside, she felt drawn to the house. But, when she called and spoke to the real estate agent, he told her he already had an offer on the house and wasn't taking any others.

Julie felt crushed, but was determined not to give up. She offered to pay a higher rent, but the agent said he couldn't accept it. This led to a long conversation, at the end of which the real estate agent commented, "It sounds as if it would be the perfect house for you." He did take her number and said maybe he could find her something else in the area.

Julie looked for other houses in the area, and even looked at one across the street, but each time she drove past the house she was drawn to it, imagining herself there. Finally, finding nothing, she made plans to move to L.A., feeling it really must be time to move on. She even gave notice, started withdrawing from her usual activities, and planned a weekend in L.A. to find a place to live. Yet she was still uncertain—she had a deep inner feeling that she really belonged in the first house. Rationally, her feeling made no sense. It was over a month since the real estate agent had told her the house was rented.

Then, a few days before her planned weekend in L.A., he called. Amazingly, the house was available again because a contractor took much longer to refurbish the house than expected and the original renters backed out. The agent had remembered their earlier conversation, and now he wanted to give her the first chance at it.

The agent drove her out to look at the house. She immediately felt that yes, she had to live here; it was the house in which she had seen herself. She decided to stay. Once Julie moved in, she made other changes in her life that helped her overcome the restlessness that led her to consider leaving San Francisco and enabled her to benefit from the many established connections she already had in the area.

For Julie the experience was a lesson in listening to and trusting that deep inner sense of knowing (her continued feeling of being drawn to the house even after she was told it wasn't available) and the correctness of the information that she gained when looking within for insights (the image she saw when she visualized where to live).

Sometimes it's hard to recognize this knowing, and sometimes obstacles may prevent us from realizing what we know, and sometimes a positive outcome may seem impossible. But Julie's experience reaffirms the importance of paying attention to our intuition and acting on it, especially when it feels so strong.

∎How to Know When Your Intuitions Are Correct

The key is to distinguish the difference in the quality and intensity of the feelings we get when our intuitions are correct and when they are not. How? By paying close attention to how you feel in both instances and noticing the differences, you can determine how your current feelings, premonitions, and beliefs compare to past patterns, and you can decide whether your intuition is correct or incorrect. Again, since intuition is subjective, there are no guarantees, but this awareness of past results will increase your chances of correctly evaluating an intuitive impulse.

The following exercise will help you look back and notice the differences.

Exercise 1

ASSESSING YOUR FEELINGS AND INSIGHTS

(Time: 10–15 minutes)

To start looking at the differences in the way you feel when your intuitive impressions are correct and when they are not, first relax. Concentrate on your breathing for about a minute. Notice it going in and out, in and out, in and out.

Now think back to a time when you had a strong feeling, premonition, or belief about something you didn't consciously know but that later turned out to be correct. Maybe you had a feeling about what someone was *really* like. . . . Maybe you had a premonition of some danger ahead. . . . Maybe you believed something about someone that later turned out to be true. Whatever it was, focus on this incident and see it happening right now. See it on the screen or area before you and watch . . .

Now, recall the feeling you had about this event before it happened. What did it feel like? Feel that feeling now. Pay attention to how it feels . . .

How intense is the feeling? If you were rating it on a scale of 0 to 100, how intense would it be? What number flashes into your mind?

Where is this feeling located? In your head? Your heart or chest? Your stomach or solar plexus? All over?

Are any images or words associated with the feeling? Any pictures? Any voices? Any memories? If so, what are they like?

Now continue to focus on feeling that feeling. Imagine for a moment you are that feeling. . . . And now, if that feeling wanted to speak to you or give you a message, what would it say? Listen to, see, or feel that. . . . Now, let go of that feeling and that incident.

Recall another time when you had a feeling, premonition, or belief about something that turned out to be correct. Again, focus on this incident and see it happening.

Again, recall the feeling you had about this event before it happened. What did it feel like? Feel that feeling now. Pay attention to how it feels . . .

How intense is the feeling? If you were rating it on a scale of 0 to 100, how intense would it be? What number flashes into your mind?

Where is this feeling located? In your head? Your heart or chest? Your stomach or solar plexus? All over?

Are any images or words associated with the feeling? Any pictures? Any voices? Any memories? If so, what are they like?

Now continue to focus on feeling that feeling. Imagine for a moment you are that feeling. . . . And now, if that feeling wanted to speak to you or give you a message, what would it say? Listen to, see, or feel that feeling. . . . Now, let go of that feeling and that incident.

Now reflect back on the two feelings you just experienced. How were they alike? How alike were they in their intensity? Where were they located? What images or words were associated with them? In what ways were they the same? Look for these similarities. They are cues you can use in the future to indicate that a feeling or insight is correct.

Now think back to a time when you had a feeling, premonition, or belief about something you didn't consciously know and that later turned out to be incorrect. Maybe you thought you knew about what someone was *really* like. . . . Maybe you had a premonition of some danger ahead. . . . Maybe you believed something about someone that later turned out to be false. Whatever it was, focus on this incident and see it happening right now. See it on the screen or area before you and watch . . .

Now, recall the feeling you had about this event before you discovered you were wrong. What did it feel like? Feel that feeling now. Pay attention to how it feels . . .

How intense is the feeling? If you were rating it on a scale of 0 to 100, how intense would it be? What number flashes into your mind?

Where is this feeling located? In your head? Your heart or chest? Your stomach or solar plexus? All over?

Are any images or words associated with the feeling? Any pictures? Any voices? Any memories? If so, what are they like?

Is there anything about the feeling that is a signal that your intuition is not correct? Is there something about its intensity, its location, the images or words associated with it that might be a cue to ignore this feeling? Now, let go of that feeling and that incident.

Recall another time when you had a feeling, premonition, or belief about something that turned out to be wrong. Again, focus on this incident and see it happening.

Again, recall the feeling you had about this event before you discovered you were incorrect. What did it feel like? Feel that feeling now. Pay attention to how it feels . . .

How intense is the feeling? If you were rating it on a scale of 0 to 100, how intense would it be? What number flashes into your mind?

Where is this feeling located? In your head? Your heart or chest? Your stomach or solar plexus? All over?

Are any images or words associated with the feeling? Any pictures? Any voices? Any memories? If so, what are they like?

Is there anything about the feeling that is a signal that your intuition is not correct? Is there something about its intensity, its location, the images or words associated with it that might be a cue to ignore this feeling? Now, let go of that feeling and that incident.

Now reflect back on the two feelings you just experienced. How were they alike? How were they alike in their intensity? Where were they located? What images or words were associated with them? In what ways were they the same? Look for these similarities. They are cues you can use in the future to indicate that a feeling or insight is incorrect and should be ignored.

Finally, reflect on the differences you just experienced in the intensity and quality of the feelings you had when you were correct and when you were incorrect. How were they different in their intensity? In where the feeling was located? In the images or words associated with them? Those differences are cues you can use in the future to tell you whether or not to pay attention to a feeling, premonition, or belief.

■Tracking Your Intuition

Another way to improve your intuitive success rate is to practice using your intuition in everyday situations, noticing the difference in the way you feel when you are correct and when you are not, and keeping a mental or written record of how well you do. Over time, you will find your ability to know when your intuition is correct will go up.

For example, you can get immediate feedback on whether your intuitions are right or wrong by trying to determine:

➤ the number of calls on your answering machine when you return to your office;

➤ the number of letters you will receive in the mail;

➤ whether a certain person will call;

➤ whether someone will cancel an appointment;

➤ whether someone will be at a certain event;

➤ whether someone will be a candidate . . . or win . . . in an election.

The possibilities are endless. You can test yourself with just about anything, though in the beginning it is best to start with less important situations. As you test yourself, notice how certain you felt you were correct and how accurate your impressions really were. Over time, both should go up. As you feel more certain about your ability, you can apply it to making decisions or setting expectations in situations that really matter. Use the chart on the following page to track your accuracy.

TRACK YOUR INTUITION SUCCESS RATIO

Impression, Belief, or Prediction	Feeling of Certainty (%)	Accuracy of Impression (Scale 0–5)
1._____		_____
2._____		_____
3._____		_____
4._____		_____
5._____		_____
6._____		_____
7._____		_____
8._____		_____
9._____		_____
10._____		_____
11._____		_____
12._____		_____
13._____		_____
14._____		_____
15._____		_____
16._____		_____
17._____		_____
18._____		_____

CHAPTER 3

UNLEASH NEW IDEAS

The Power of Focused Perception and Brainstorming

*T*o use and apply these creative-force techniques effectively, you need a little preparation and practice. In time, they will become second nature and you will use them every day, like anything else that has become a part of your life.

The process involves developing your ability to access your inner powers in two ways:

1. look within in a focused way, so you can become aware of your inner knowledge and power;

2. let go of your critical judge, analytical thinking or habitual way of looking at things so you can freely come up with new ideas.

Then, as you become adept at getting in touch with this information and at generating ideas, you can draw on these abilities to do more and more things you want to do.

■Accessing Your Inner Knowledge

The hardest thing about getting insights from within is learning to tune out that rational thought and self-talk we hear much of the time. We have to learn to listen very carefully; we have to focus our attention on that very low, quiet message; otherwise it can easily be drowned out.

Then, too, we have to know what form the message is coming in, so when we pay attention, we are better able to perceive it. For example, *listening* to that message is just one way to perceive it. *Seeing* pictures or images of your inner messages is another. Or perhaps you may experience *feelings* or *sensations* or even have a *feeling of knowing* that signals a communication from your inner source of knowledge. Or sometimes you may get these messages from multiple channels at once—especially when the message is especially powerful and important for you.

However you perceive your inner messages, you must know what to pay attention to and what to screen out. It's a little different in each case. If the information is conveyed in pictures or images, you must determine which pictures or images are accurate, and which to ignore. If you experience feelings or sensations, the question is what types of feelings or sensations deserve serious attention and which do not. If you have a sense of knowing, what is there about that knowing that means it is really true or not?

The chart on page 29 summarizes these different methods of gaining inner knowledge. It also shows you what to screen out and what to look for to determine if this knowledge is accurate.

Thus, the first step to using this inner information is to recognize the form in which you are most likely to receive it to determine whether or not the information you receive is accurate. Should you receive this information on multiple channels—and you can learn to develop this ability by practicing developing your different modes of perception (Exercise 4, page 33)—that can sometimes help confirm that the insight is correct, much like hearing the same report on different radio stations. Whatever channel or channels you receive the message on, the original source of the message could be wrong, so you have to learn to verify the message. You have to refine your ability to *really* know what

HOW DO YOU PERCEIVE INNER KNOWLEDGE?
HOW TO KNOW WHEN IT'S ACCURATE

Mode of Perception	Characteristics	Outside Interference	Signs of Accuracy
Visual Orientation	Pictures, symbols, images; like seeing scenes in a film.	False stereotypes, inaccurate pictures, wrong interpretations of symbols.	Intensity and clarity of image; intensity of knowing interpretation is correct; repetition of image.
Auditory Orientation	Words, sounds, voices; like listening to a radio program.	Competing thoughts or voices; words of parents or others about how things are.	Intensity and clarity of message; intensity of knowing message correct; repetition of message.
Feeling Orientation	Feelings or sensations; like experiencing a strong tension pulling or touching in one's body.	Competing feelings or emotions; negative feelings (such as being anxious or angry) that throw one's perceptions of feelings off.	Intensity and strength of feeling or sensation; intensity of knowing feeling is accurate; repetition of feeling or sensation.
Knowing Orientation	Sense of knowing or awareness that something is true; like a flash of light or illumination.	Feelings of uncertainty or confusion; a lack of confidence in one's abilities to know.	Intensity and strength of sense of knowing; bright or focused quality of sense of light or illumination.

you know—and usually the way to do this is by noticing the intensity, volume, and clarity of the message. The stronger, clearer, and more focused it is—whether it's an image, voice, feeling, or sense of knowing—the more likely it is to be correct.

■How to Touch with the Four Sensory Modes

How do you get this inner information yourself? How perceptive and accurate are you in each of these four areas: seeing, hearing, feeling or sensing, and knowing? The following exercises will help you discover how you get information and how accurate it is.

Exercise 2 will help you identify your primary sources of information and analyze how strong and accurate your insights in each mode of perception are. As you do the exercise, record what you experience. Use the form (page 31) to record this information. This will give you a baseline to assess how keen your abilities are in each area. Once you establish this baseline, you can practice developing your abilities using Exercise 4. Retest yourself from time to time to see how you are improving.

Exercise 2

DISCOVERING YOUR PRIMARY MODE
FOR GETTING INFORMATION

(Time: 5–10 minutes)

Begin by getting in a relaxed, calm state in a quiet place. Do a little deep breathing with your eyes closed until you feel totally relaxed and have emptied your mind of outside information and thoughts. Then, in this receptive frame of mind, ask yourself: Give me an idea or experience. Now, without trying to shape or control whatever happens, notice what occurs. Do you see something? Does an image or scene appear? Do you experience thoughts, voices, or sounds? Do you notice feelings or sensations? Do you experience some sort of light or illumination? Or do you experience a combination of perceptions?

Whatever you experience is likely to be your primary way of receiving information. Make a note—you can record this on the top half of the form on page 31 (make a copy first so you can use this form again)— under the heading Primary Quality. Next to the number 1, enter whichever mode seemed strongest to you first, followed by any other qualities in their apparent order of strength.

Then, ask this question again: Give me another idea or experience. And again, let an experience occur without trying to consciously create it. Then note how you primarily perceived it next to the number 2.

Try this process five times, noting your mode of perception next to the numbers 3, 4, and 5, and see if the same mode of perception is repeated. If so, that suggests that it is a very strong mode of perception for you. If you have different modes of perception or a combination of modes each time, this suggests you are likely to have a mixed way of perceiving information.

MY MAJOR MODES OF PERCEPTION
AND THEIR ACCURACY

Note: Copy this form for use with exercises 2 and 3.

Primary Quality: (strongest mode of perception)	*Secondary Quality:* (next strongest mode of perception, if any)	*Other Quality* (additional modes of perception, if any)
1._____	1._____	1._____
2._____	2._____	2._____
3._____	3._____	3._____
4._____	4._____	4._____
5._____	5._____	5._____

Quality	*Strength of Quality*	*Accuracy of Quality*
Visual Perception	_____	_____
Auditory Perception	_____	_____
Feeling Perception	_____	_____
Knowing Perception	_____	_____

Now, having a sense of how you primarily receive information from your inner self or intuition, try assessing how strong and accurate your perceptions are in each mode. Commonly, you will find that your perceptual abilities are strongest and most accurate in your primary mode, although this is not always the case. Also, your abilities can vary in their strength and accuracy at different times, depending on how you feel and how focused you are. Then, too, with practice, you can increase the strength and accuracy of these different abilities, so that if you are weak in certain areas you can improve to become more balanced in the ways in which you get your intuitive knowledge. Use Exercise 3 to rate your abilities now; later, you can rate yourself again to see how your abilities may have changed—and have usually improved—with practice.

Exercise 3

DETERMINING THE STRENGTH AND ACCURACY OF YOUR MODES OF PERCEPTION

(Time: 3–5 minutes)

Again, close your eyes and get very relaxed. Breathe deeply and empty your mind of all thoughts. Tell yourself you will be receptive to whatever information comes. Then, for each of the four perceptual qualities, ask yourself: How strong is my ability to perceive in this way on a scale of 0 to 100? Afterwards, notice the first number that comes into your mind—whether you see it, hear it, feel it, or know it. Write it down on the appropriate line on the bottom half of the form on page 31 under "Strength of Quality." That should give you a sense of the average intensity of a particular perceptive sense. Later, you can use the same test to gauge the intensity of a particular bit of information that comes to you about something you want to know.

Next, find out how accurate the information you receive in this way usually is. To do so, for each of the four perceptual qualities, ask yourself: How accurate is my ability to perceive in this way on a scale of 0 to 100? Again, notice the first number that comes into your mind, however it does, and write it down on the appropriate line under "Accuracy of Quality." This will give you a sense of the probability that a perception is accurate on the average. Likewise, you can use this test to gauge the accuracy of a particular insight you have received.

You can improve your ability to gain information from your other modes of perception through the practice of developing them. The more you work with your perception, the more you use it, the more it improves. If you are already very strong in one perceptual mode, it can prevent you from developing another, because it comes to the fore so quickly and takes over. But if you deliberately work to inhibit your primary mode, you can improve the others. Your primary mode will continue to be strong and ready when you want it, because your skill with this part of yourself has been developed for so long it has become second nature.

Exercise 4

DEVELOPING YOUR SECONDARY MODES OF PERCEPTION

(Time: 5–10 minutes)

To develop these other perceptual skills you can either

- select one other skill to develop, or
- work on developing two or all three of your other skills simultaneously.

Then, do the following.

Close your eyes and get into a very relaxed state. Then, ask yourself a question about something you want to gain some insight into. Ask to get this information in your usual (or primary) mode of getting information, such as:

Where should I go on my vacation? (Give me a picture, tell me, give me a feeling, let me know).

What kind of job should I seek? (Give me a picture, tell me, give me a feeling, let me know).

Then, notice how the information comes—do you *see* the image of where you will be going or what your new job will look like; do you *hear* a voice telling you what to do; do you get a *feeling* or *sensation* that tells you this is really what you want to do; do you *know* that this is what will actually happen. In most cases, you will get the answer in your primary mode, in the way you have asked to get it. If you don't, just note it. You'll probably want to work on strengthening this ability too.

Now, having gotten the information in one mode, ask to get it in another—either the single way you have chosen to practice, or in sequence in each of the other ways you want to develop. For example, if you have *seen* an image of something (where you would like to take your vacation, your dream job), ask to *hear* a voice telling you the same thing, ask to *feel* a sensation in your abdomen or elsewhere in your body that indicates this is what you should do; ask to get a *sense of knowing* that you are making the right choice. Then, concentrate on getting this perception in this different way. If your primary mode of perceiving interferes and gives you another response (for example, if your sense of vision is very strong, you may get another picture; or if your auditory mode is powerful, you may hear another reassuring voice telling you the answer), turn your attention away from that perception and ask to get the response again in another mode, and then be receptive. Do this several times, if necessary, until you experience this other mode of perception. Then, once you do, ask additional questions, and try to get a response in this other mode. If you continue to perceive answers in your primary mode, repeat the process of pushing that perception away and ask for a response in this other way.

As you practice, you should find that perceiving in your other modes becomes easier.

Initially, it's easier to develop one perceptual skill at a time. But as the process becomes easier to work with, you can ask to get this information in various modes in sequence. As you practice, not only will you get better at using these different modes, but you'll find you can more readily draw on the perceptual mode you want or you can seek information through multiple channels. This will help to reinforce the information you are getting and your confidence in its correctness.

∎The Power of Brainstorming to Release Your Creative Potential

Besides failing to look within to perceive insights, our internal critical judge and old habit patterns can be major blocks to discovering new ideas and possibilities. To release our creative powers, we need to be able to let them go. If we can let go of this analytic, judgmental part of our nature and put aside our usual ways of doing or viewing things, we can let our inner creativity break through.

Brainstorming, which is usually done in groups, provides a good model for this process of letting go and breaking out of old patterns. In the first phase of the process, the group is asked to come up with ideas in a kind of idea free-for-all. People are urged to shout out ideas as they come to mind (while someone records them), and to avoid criticizing, analyzing, or evaluating. The purpose of this approach is to prevent that internal critic from stepping in and making the participants think about what they are saying and making them fear being judged, which would inhibit or abort the process of coming up with new ideas. Later, in the next phase, the ideas are evaluated and those considered the best can be further developed or adopted.

A similar process can be used individually to promote creative insights and solutions. It can help us get unstuck from the way things are and help us come up with new alternatives, answers, and possibilities. It can help us overcome undesirable habits and ways of doing things, and it can help us discover new ways to accomplish our goals.

Brainstorm to Generate New Ideas

Use brainstorming when you feel stuck or uncertain about what to do—shake yourself out of your rut and generate alternative possibilities from which to choose. For example, consider brainstorming when

> ➤ you feel hemmed in by too many everyday responsibilities and are seeking ways out of the trap;

> ➤ you want to change jobs or move into a new field, but aren't sure what exactly you want to do;

> ➤ you want to do something different in your life, such as move to a new town, take a trip, buy a car, take up a new hobby, find new friends—but you aren't sure what you want;

> ➤ you haven't been able to lose weight on any diet program you have tried and want a new approach that really works.

Whatever the problem, brainstorming can shake you out of old habits and patterns to maximize your alternatives. Then you can decide on the best possibility for you.

Take, for example, Suzanna, a woman in her early forties. She has been drifting away from her husband for years. They have been married about twenty years, have two teenaged children (who are away for most of the year at school or camp). As husband and wife they live largely separate lives. He often travels out of the country, and she spends much of her time working and going to business and professional parties. What's more, she is disturbed by the superficiality of the people she meets, most of whom seem overly concerned with appearances and uninterested in making a commitment to anyone else. While she has a good career in her own financial-planning business and could easily do whatever she wants, her ties to her husband have held her back. Year after year she has considered leaving, or not leaving, her husband. Their arrangement is comfortable, but she feels frustrated and blocked. Should she stay married and remain where she is; should she move to the country to which her husband usually travels; or should they break up? Unsure of what to do, uncertain about change, she has stuck to—and remained stuck in—the tried and true.

Such an approach is common. It's easier, safer to do what's known. But this very ease and comfort can be a barrier to trying new, more satisfying ways of doing things. We don't look—or we are afraid to. However, once we do, we can be open to discovering new possibilities. Brainstorming allows us to actively generate all sorts of alternatives to consider.

Suzanna, for example, might brainstorm in two phases: First, she could consider all the things she might like to do if she stayed married and what she might do to revitalize her marriage. Then she could rationally decide which factors are most important to her and come to a decision. Second, since she is also feeling dissatisfied with other aspects of her life, she might think about alternative activities and replace those she doesn't like with what she really wants to do. In short, by imagining the possibilities and selecting some to act on, Suzanna could change her situation and create a more satisfying life.

Consider how you might use brainstorming to discover new options and alternatives that might help you attain a goal or be more productive or earn more. I frequently use this approach to develop new ideas for projects. For example, when I design games, I might look at some materials around the house, such as a plastic sphere and stove bolts, ask myself: "How can I use these materials in a game or puzzle?" and visualize the different ways to do so. (In this case, the idea became a puzzle called "Screwball," published by Hasbro.) In other cases, I have started with a theme and asked myself something like, "What games can I invent relating to current events?" (This one turned into a game called "Get a Job!", published by Microcosm.) Or I might try the same process with a particular market in mind, such as a game for girls aged six to ten. Then, after asking my question, I just put my conscious self out of the way and let the ideas flow.

■How to Brainstorm for Maximum Results

As in groups, the basic way to brainstorm is to divide the process into two phases. In the first, you want to come up with as many alternative ideas, suggestions, approaches, or solutions as you can as quickly as possible. In the second, you choose the most appropriate or interesting ideas, and then expand on or implement them.

The process is ideal for increasing creativity and unblocking old habit patterns, because it stimulates your mind to start generating new ideas and solutions without the restrictions that come from critically evaluating them. It's like telling your critical judge to take a vacation, so you can experiment or explore. There's no internal critic stepping in to say: "No, that's wrong" or "What a stupid idea!" Then, after you've come up with the ideas, you can let your judge out to review them—to decide objectively what seems good or bad, preferable or not. This review process can involve critically eliminating those ideas that don't work and prioritizing those that are possible.

If you have trouble logically deciding what to do, this might be the time to look within to see what ideas you most respond to on the intuitive level—what looks, sounds, feels, or on a gut level you know is right.

In short, effective brainstorming is a two-stage process, in which the second—deciding—phase can be done either rationally or intuitively.

Stage 1—To generate ideas quickly without the interference of the conscious, rational, critical mind;

Stage 2—To review and select the best ideas in one of two ways:

1. Calling on your internal critic to rationally evaluate, rate, and prioritize these ideas;

2. Calling on your inner knowledge or wisdom to intuitively select the ideas you want to pursue, based on what you see, hear, feel, or know.

■Brainstorming Stage 1: Create a Powerful Focus

To brainstorm effectively, you need clarity and focus. You need to know very specifically what the problem or issue is.

Second, you need time. In some simple situations, you can come up with a variety of viable alternatives and choose among them in just a few minutes. In fact, as you get good at brainstorming, you can short-circuit the formal process described here, which takes about 5 to 10 minutes, and do it all mentally in about 2 to 3 minutes. But in more complex situations, where there are many problems and issues to be considered, allow additional time, perhaps 20 to 30 minutes or even more, to really focus on and think of possibilities.

As you prepare to brainstorm, clarify the problem or issue so it is concrete and specific. Avoid vague questions. A question such as "What should I do with my life?" is too vague. Narrow the question to something more focused, like: "What type of career would I like to pursue in the next five years?" or "What personality traits do I need to develop to improve my ability to get along with people and persuade them to follow my leadership?" Or, even more specifically, you might ask something like, "Where should I go on my vacation this summer?"

In some cases, this process of refining the question and making it more concrete and specific may mean you can divide up one broad and vague question into several specific parts and then brainstorm ideas for each part. For example, a question like "What kind of position in a new field do I want to find next?" might be divided into these separate topics: "What type of industry do I want to get into? . . . What type of company within this industry do I want to work for? . . . What type of work do I want to do in this company?"

If you have your question clearly in mind before you get into the relaxed state necessary for brainstorming, start there. If you don't, take some time to clarify the question you want to ask. Get into a relaxed state and ask yourself, "What question or topic do I want to brainstorm about?" Then, notice what question comes into your mind, and if the question seems too general, ask for a further clarification, until you have a specific clear question or series of questions to ask in the brainstorming process.

With your question clarified and focused, you are ready to begin the brainstorming process.

Exercise 5

PERSONAL BRAINSTORMING TO GENERATE IDEAS

(Time: 5–10 minutes)

Now, with your question in mind or written down, and in a relaxed state in a quiet place, ask your question. Have a sheet of paper and a pencil ready, so you can write down the ideas as you think of them.

Then, go. Don't try to judge, analyze, or criticize. Allow yourself to come up with any ideas, however strange, silly, impractical, or outlandish they seem, as quickly as you can. Write them down, giving equal weight to each one. Regardless of the nature of the idea, don't evaluate or critique it. Any analysis or review will snap you out of this creative idea-generating mode. The idea is to be both active and receptive simultaneously—active in quickly generating ideas and receptive in accepting enthusiastically whatever comes.

Make copies of the Brainstorming form on page 41 and use it to write down ideas When you write using this approach, it's as if you are on automatic pilot (this writing process is sometimes called "automatic writing"); after awhile your thoughts may automatically trigger your writing without your even telling yourself to do so. In turn, this process of writing things down automatically will help you generate more ideas, since such writing itself serves as an imagination trigger. The more you use this free-flowing process, the freer you will find your mind becomes. Your intuitive, imaginative processes will be loosened up, and one idea will help trigger another.

Even if the ideas don't come at first, which sometimes happens when you start brainstorming, continue focusing on the problem. Then, whenever an idea pops into your mind, even if it's just the wispy fragment of an idea, write it down. Just focusing on the problem or issue will help to get the process going. Then, once it starts, the triggering effect will lead to new ideas.

Continue as long as the ideas keep flowing freely. When the ideas slow down, allow about a minute or two at the end for any final thoughts, perhaps saying to yourself: "Can I think of any more ideas on this question?" Then, in the same receptive state of mind, wait to see if any more ideas come. Finally, when you feel that you have stopped thinking of new ideas and the process is complete, stop.

The Power of Brainstorming with a Group to Stimulate Change

Brainstorming in a group can be a good source of new ideas, especially if you're feeling blocked. Getting ideas from others can be a stimulus to change.

The basic process is the same—there are two stages—the initial creative idea-producing phase in which you come up with ideas and the review and analysis phase to select ideas. In a group, if you feel blocked, let the others take the lead. Remain silent and listen until you feel inspired by the process to join in, and be sure to avoid any "yes, buts" if others suggest ideas you already considered but discarded. As the ideas pour out, you or someone else in the group should write them down.

BRAINSTORMING—
IDEAS AND ALTERNATIVES

Note: Copy this form for use with exercises 5, 6, and 7.

My question is:_____

	How I Rate
Some possible alternatives, solutions, or ideas	*These Ideas*
for answering this are:	*(scale 0–5)*

1._____

2._____

3._____

4._____

5._____

6._____

7._____

8._____

9._____

10._____

11._____

12._____

13._____

14._____

15._____

16._____

Exercise 6 _____

GROUP BRAINSTORMING TO GENERATE IDEAS

(Time: 10–20 minutes)

The guidelines for brainstorming are identical: Start the process with a clear specific question. In the first stage neither you nor the others should criticize or judge the ideas proposed. You can piggyback or expand on what's been suggested but should not analyze or evaluate the ideas. You should avoid any temptation to interrupt or comment— explaining how you tried something before, why you think something won't work, will only shortcircuit the process and make others reluctant to make suggestions. Even if something seems stupid or outrageous, write it down. In the second stage, when you review and evaluate, you can always edit out these suggestions; you may even find the germ of a good idea in one that at first seemed silly.

Keep the process going as long as the ideas keep coming, and when the process slows down, ask others if they can think of any more ideas. Then, see if anything else comes up.

Plan on about 10 to 20 minutes for the process, but allow it to go a little longer if people are really being creative. Select a place where everyone can focus on the problem without distractions. Everyone should be agreeable to participating and staying focused on the question you want to brainstorm.

It's up to you to review and select from the list suggested by others.

_____

∎Brainstorming Stage 2: Make the Right Choices

Once you have your list of possible ideas, decide which ones you like best, using whatever criteria are appropriate for the particular situation. For example, determine which are the most workable, the most creative, the most profitable.

Exercise 7

REVIEWING AND SELECTING IDEAS

Using the form on page 41, go down your list and quickly give each idea a rating from 0 (terrible) to 5 (tops) to indicate how much you like that idea. If you're not sure or think an idea has possibilities, but needs some more development through additional brainstorming, place a (?) in the rating column.

When you rate your ideas, let your intuitive mind respond automatically. Don't try to assess each idea logically. Then, review your top-rated ideas. Generally, these are the ones to start working with and implementing first. If there are too many to be implemented at once, rate this top group again and begin with the top-rated ideas from this new list.

How to Handle Conflicting Needs

Often the review process is straightforward, and you can easily react to and rate your options. But what if you have conflicting needs—each of which is important to you? For example, in deciding whether or not to take a job, both your interest in the work and the rate of pay may be important needs.

Exercise 8

ASSESSING CONFLICTING NEEDS

When faced with conflicting needs, the same brainstorming process can help you come up with ideas and the same critical-intuitive process can help you rate them. Each choice should be rated separately for each conflicting need. If the two considerations are of equal importance to you, you can average them together. If one need is more important than another, weight them accordingly and factor this greater weight into the averaging process. One way to do this is to weight each need on a scale of 1 to 5 and multiply each of the ratings by that weighting.

Then compare these weighted ratings to select the options you most prefer, taking both needs into consideration.

For example, say it's much more important to have a job that is interesting to you and offers the opportunity to gain new skills and knowledge than it is to have a job that pays well. You might give "interest" a weight of 5. Yet, you still want a job that pays reasonably well—you don't want to sacrifice all. Perhaps, give "pay" a 3. Then, when you are faced with alternative job choices, rate each one on how interesting it is and how well it pays. Then, multiply these ratings by the weightings, add together, and divide by 2 to come up with an average.

If there are additional criteria, simply add ratings for them; use the weighting process if any of them is more important than the others and figure out an average score for each alternative. (Thus, if you have 3 needs, you will multiply these 3 ratings by each of the 3 weightings and divide by 3 to come up with an average). Finally, after you have appropriately averaged and, if necessary, weighted each alternative, you can select those options that have the highest ratings.

You can use the exercise form on the following page for brainstorming and rating options when you have one or more conflicting criteria affecting your choice.

To use the form, list each of the conflicting criteria you are considering as Factor #1, Factor #2, and so forth. List the weight you have given that factor for as many alternatives as you are considering. Then, rate the alternative, and enter that number for each of the factors you have listed. Now multiply the rating and the weight for each factor to get a total. Finally, add up that total, divide by the number of factors, and enter the result for that alternative in the column that says: "Average Rating. (See page 45 to see how the form would have been filled out for the job decision described above.)

■How to Use Brainstorming in Your Business and Personal Life

As you can see, the uses for brainstorming are literally endless. Here are two examples:

Renegotiate a Contract. One woman found the process useful in dealing with tenants. She wanted them to move so she

ASSESSING CONFLICTING NEEDS

Note: Copy this form for use with exercise 8.

My Question, Problem, or Goal is: _____

Possible Alternatives	Factor #1				Factor #2				Factor #3				Average Rating
	Rtg	×	Wgt	= Tot	Rtg	×	Wgt	= Tot	Rtg	×	Wgt	= Tot	
1. _____	—	—	—	—	—	—	—	—	—	—	—	—	—
2. _____	—	—	—	—	—	—	—	—	—	—	—	—	—
3. _____	—	—	—	—	—	—	—	—	—	—	—	—	—
4. _____	—	—	—	—	—	—	—	—	—	—	—	—	—
5. _____	—	—	—	—	—	—	—	—	—	—	—	—	—
6. _____	—	—	—	—	—	—	—	—	—	—	—	—	—
7. _____	—	—	—	—	—	—	—	—	—	—	—	—	—
8. _____	—	—	—	—	—	—	—	—	—	—	—	—	—
9. _____	—	—	—	—	—	—	—	—	—	—	—	—	—
10. _____	—	—	—	—	—	—	—	—	—	—	—	—	—
11. _____	—	—	—	—	—	—	—	—	—	—	—	—	—
12. _____	—	—	—	—	—	—	—	—	—	—	—	—	—

could sell the property, but she couldn't legally do so, since their lease included an option to renew. She felt stuck, but in brainstorming, a number of options came up: "Help them find a new place, and give them a bonus for moving. . . ." "Offer a refund on their rent for a few months if they move. . . ." "Give them a percentage of the sale price of the property if they agree to move if the property is sold. . . ." "Explain the situation to them and let them know their new landlord won't be so accommodating if they choose to stay. . . ." Then, armed with a few of the more reasonable possibilities, she went off to talk to her tenants and found a compromise that worked for all of them.

Plan a More Interesting Party. Another woman used the process to avoid having just another cocktail-party mixer for singles. How could she make it different? After brainstorming, she had all sorts of choices: "Ask the attendees each to bring an old boyfriend or girlfriend, so there's an equal balance. . . ." "Try some games to get people acquainted. . . ." "Ask each person to bring a unique dish and explain what's special about it. . . ." "Put other people's name tags on guests and have them try to find their own names. . . ."

Now fill in your own question and try brainstorming yourself. You can use it for virtually anything, including:

➤ planning events;

➤ making job and career choices;

➤ selecting projects to undertake;

➤ resolving serious personal problems;

➤ and (fill in your own purposes).

▮Brainstorming Bonus: Implement Your Ideas

Besides using brainstorming to make decisions and come up with alternate ideas, you can also brainstorm to determine how to implement an idea. Suppose after brainstorming about a career move you have come up with several possibilities and have chosen one. You might next want to brainstorm something like, "How do I go about finding such a job?" Or suppose you decided where to go on your next vacation, your next question might be, "How do I finance the trip?" or "How can I put together a group, so I can get a free trip?"

You can also use brainstorming to develop the steps you need to turn an idea into a reality. For instance, you might break these down into several categories—the methods to use, the people or groups you need, and the objects required to make the goal a reality—and then ask a question about each through the brain-storming process.

The Four-Step Review Process

In short, you can use the review process by itself or with additional brainstorming to:

1. Set priorities—list of the possibilities and alternatives and choose among them.
2. Select ideas for further development through more brain-storming.
3. Come up with even more specific alternatives.
4. Decide what you need or what to do to implement your ideas.

Put Your Ideas into Action

Once you have determined that something is a high priority for you and you want to do it, whether you have used the process of focused perception or brainstorming, it's time to put your ideas into action.

A good way to start is by creating a timeline indicating a date for completing the project or achieving the goal. If possible, set the dates to begin within a few days or at most a week after making the decision to avoid letting them slide. If you realistically know you can't act on an alternative until a certain time, set a future date, commit yourself to it, and provide a reminder for yourself that this date is coming up (such as marking your calendar).

You can help solidify your commitment to act if you announce your plan to someone else—a spouse, friend, or associate—by publicly committing yourself to action. Telling someone of your plan can give you a sense of support for what you are doing. After you have accomplished your goal, telling that person can give you further incentive to move on to other plans, in response to the praise or recognition you will get for your achievement.

For example, at a meeting on managing time, we each went through the process of personally brainstorming all the things we had been procrastinating about. After we decided what was most important to us, we were asked to tell our plans and the date on which we would take action to the person next to us. The woman next to me announced that she had long been wanting to sign up for dancing classes, but had been putting it off. Now she planned to do something about it in a few days. I told her that I planned to organize my office by the end of the month. The following week she called to say she had started her lessons, and I told her I had started working on my office, too. For each of us, the decision to set a date, coupled with telling someone else of our plan, contributed to our motivation to act.

Develop an Action Plan

In summary, after you generate ideas, set priorities, and decide what you want to do, come up with a plan of action and decide when you are going to implement it by setting a date and writing it down. Telling someone can help reinforce your commitment. (You might even ask that person to call you to remind you of it.) Use the Action Plan form on page 49 to help guide you. On it, you can list a dozen possibilities (you can add more or use fewer depending on your needs). Enter a start date in the column headed "Date to Begin" and enter an estimated completion date in the column headed "Date to Complete." Though you can change these dates, they provide a guideline for where you are going.

Finally, when the dates arrive, go ahead and take action, assuming your planned action is still important to you. Things change, so ask yourself: "Do I still really want to do this?" Use your inner feelings to help you decide. Then, if it still seems right, avoid excuses, "Yes, buts" and "I'll do it laters." Do it now!

MY ACTION PLAN

Possibilities I Want to Act On	Date to Begin	Date to Complete
1._____	_____	_____
2._____	_____	_____
3._____	_____	_____
4._____	_____	_____
5._____	_____	_____
6._____	_____	_____
7._____	_____	_____
8._____	_____	_____
9._____	_____	_____
10._____	_____	_____
11._____	_____	_____
12._____	_____	_____

∎When *Not* to Brainstorm

Brainstorming can be a time-consuming process and should be used wisely. There's no need to create choices when the choices you have made are working well and you feel good about them. In fact, brainstorming just to create more choices can be disruptive, since we all need some set routines and patterns. If we opened everything up to question, life would become too chaotic and confusing. Brainstorming is best used when focused on specific problems and issues, where alternatives will help you make changes, better choices, and decisions.

CHAPTER 4

NATURAL ENERGY BOOSTERS
Do More, Enjoy More

*T*oday, many people are taking nutrients and "smart" drinks (usually a mixture of fruit juices and proteins, vitamins, minerals, and other nutrients) to increase their energy. Why? So they can get more tasks done more quickly—perform better on a test—think faster—plow through a pile of work with more enthusiasm—for all sorts of reasons.

Those things are fine, but do you know you can charge up your energy using the power of your mind alone? Some research even suggests that by changing how you think you affect your own brain chemistry, so that your mind itself can produce its own energy-stimulating chemicals. So, forget drugs and energy enhancers. You can mentally increase your energy using only the positive power of your mind.

■Charge Yourself Up—Mentally

You can undoubtedly think of many times when you want more energy to do all the things you want or need to do. We all experience situations when we need an extra energy boost to keep us going. While certain chemical boosters (like the caffeine that comes with those extra cups of coffee) can help, too much can cause negative side effects (and even create addictions). Instead, charge yourself up mentally; empower your mind naturally.

A mental charge can be especially useful in times like these:

➤ You feel generally tired or sleepy during the day and can't take a nap.

➤ You have a series of important deadlines to meet.

➤ You are resisting working on a project because it feels too big or overwhelming, and you need to increase your energy to get going on it.

➤ You need to be extra enthusiastic and energetic—for a job interview, a presentation, or leading a meeting, for example.

➤ You have a difficult task—a confrontation with your boss or an employee—and you need that extra shot of energy to do it well.

When do you need more energy? Exercise 9 will help you determine those times when you normally need an energy boost. Use the form on page 54 to list those situations and to set priorities.

Exercise 9

RECOGNIZING WHEN YOU NEED AN ENERGY BOOST

(Time: 5–10 minutes)

Find a comfortable place where you can relax and still write. Then take a couple of minutes to relax. Focus on your breathing going in and out, in and out, and feel yourself calming down.

Now, fully relaxed, ask yourself this question: "When do I want or need more energy for what I am doing or want to do?" Let the answers come to you. See the situations in which you want or need more energy appear on your mental screen. How will you use this extra energy? What will you do? How will it help you in doing whatever you are doing?

As you observe each different situation, write it down. Then, ask your question again and notice the next situation that comes to you and write it down. Keep going until the situations stop coming or you feel complete.

Then, when you feel ready, return to the room. Count backwards from 5 to 1 and feel yourself coming back. Five, returning to the room. Four, three, almost back. Two. You're waking up now. And one. You're back in the room.

Review your list. Set priorities: In which situations do you feel it's most important to increase your energy level? Rate them on a scale of 0 to 5. You can use those priorities to focus on increasing your energy for the most important situations first.

■How Natural Energy Boosters Work

Each thought is a kind of electrical charge of energy that courses through your brain cells, activating neurotransmitters and other chemicals. The more focused you are in your thinking, the more energy goes through the system. It's very like directing a hose at something. Increase the pressure enough, and the water goes much further, much faster.

Thus, anything you do to concentrate and direct your thoughts can help to raise your energy level, and because of the close mind-body connection, as your mental energy increases, so will your physical energy. This relationship between mental and physical energy can be readily measured using a biofeedback device, which monitors the way the brain functions. For example, when we are at rest, asleep, or meditating, our thoughts are moving more slowly, and this is reflected in the lower frequency theta, delta, and alpha waves associated with these states. By contrast, when we are more active and alert, the feedback machine registers the faster beta wave frequencies. When we dream, the stepped-up energy of our thoughts and visual input is reflected in the faster REM waves associated with dreaming.

We can up our own energy levels by thinking high-energy thoughts or stimulating our feelings to make us more aware and alert. These thoughts and feelings change the brain and body chemistry so that we not only think we are more energetic (or feel we are), but we *actually* are more physically energized.

ASSESSING MY ENERGY NEEDS

Situations Where I Need More Energy	*Priority* *(Scale 0–5)*
1. _____	_____
2. _____	_____
3. _____	_____
4. _____	_____
5. _____	_____
6. _____	_____
7. _____	_____
8. _____	_____
9. _____	_____
10. _____	_____
11. _____	_____
12. _____	_____
13. _____	_____
14. _____	_____
15. _____	_____
16. _____	_____
17. _____	_____
18. _____	_____
19. _____	_____

Three Mental Energy Boosting Exercises

The following energy-boosting exercises are alternative ways of focusing the mind to increase your mental, emotional, and physical energy level. The first involves drawing on the energy from the experience of past situations where you have felt high energy; another involves imagining you have more energy in the specific situation you are in; and the third involves drawing generally on the energy of the environment around you. Use the approach that works best for you, or, if you like, use a combination of these techniques to raise your own energy.

Exercise 10

TAPPING INTO YOUR NATURAL ENERGY BOOSTERS

(Time: 3–5 minutes)

1. Drawing on Past Energy

In this exercise, you will imagine a situation in your past in which you have experienced a high level of energy. Then, you will imagine yourself now having this same energy to deal with a current situation.

Get relaxed in a quiet place. Focus on your breathing going in and out, in and out, until you have calmed down and feel completely relaxed.

Now, imagine yourself traveling back in the past to a time when you were especially energetic. Just see yourself going back, back, on an elevator or train back in time; when you arrive, you step into a situation where you felt especially active and full of energy. Maybe it was a social occasion, an event you attended, someplace special you went. Whatever it is, just see yourself there now and experience that sense of high energy and excitement.

Take a few minutes. Feel the strength and power of that high energy and excitement. You feel very excited, very alert, very charged . . .

Now, keeping that feeling of high energy in mind, come back into the room. Now you can take that energy and use it—you will feel full of energy, excited, very alert, and ready to do whatever you want to do.

(Time: 2–3 minutes)

2. Imagining High Energy

In this exercise, you focus on increasing your level of energy in the present situation—either just before doing something or by taking a break during the experience to recharge your energy batteries.

Find a quiet place to get relaxed—or tune out whatever is going on around you. Then, focus on your breathing going in and out, in and out, until you have calmed down and feel completely relaxed.

Now, picture the situation you are about to enter—or from which you've just taken a break. Imagine yourself having great confidence and resolve. You feel you know exactly what to say; exactly what to do; you feel very good, very sure of yourself.

Take a moment to notice whatever it is you are going to do. Imagine yourself interacting with others, playing the scene. As you do, notice you are feeling more and more energetic; more and more enthusiastic. Your feeling of ease as you relate to others or engage in this activity helps you feel very focused, very alert. You feel very charged up, excited, raring to go.

Now take a few moments just to feel that energy, alertness, and enthusiasm rising up in you. Feel it spreading through you. Through your arms, your legs, your torso, your head. You feel as if you're just radiating, glowing with energy.

Now, keeping that feeling of high energy in mind, come back into the room. Now you can go right into the situation, taking that high energy with you. You feel full of energy, excited, very alert, ready to plunge right in and do whatever you have to do.

(Time: 3–5 minutes)

3. Drawing on the Energies of the Earth and Universe

In this exercise, you imagine the energy of the earth and the surrounding universe coursing through you to give you the energy you need to do something you want to do. It's one of the most powerful general-purpose techniques for raising and directing energy.

Start by getting relaxed with your eyes closed, but this time, sit up straight, with your feet on the floor and your hands up in a receptive position.

Begin by focusing on the earth under your feet. Imagine that the earth is pulsing with energy and feel that energy flowing, like a rushing river. Feel this energy concentrating in a radiating ball right under your feet. Feel it rising up through the earth and surging into your feet and into your body. Notice how it rises through your feet, through your legs, to the base of your spine. Feel it warming and charging you as it rises. Feel it expand out through your torso, into your arms and head. Feel it giving you its strength and power as it spreads through you.

Then, as this energy continues to pour into you, notice that the energy of the universe or atmosphere around you is focusing in a ball of bright, radiant, pulsing energy at the top of your head. Now experience this energy coming in through the top of your head. You can see and feel it pouring in, and you feel it energizing you as it does. Next, experience that energy traveling through your head into your spine, into your arms, and spiraling down your torso. It feels light, airy, and expansive.

Now, focus on the two energies meeting at the base of your spine; experience the heightened charge of these two energies—the energy of the earth charging you with strength and power; the energy of the universe charging you with its feeling of lightness and expansion. Notice how they merge and blend and spiral together—like a big bright pulsing ball of energy. Experience them moving up and down your spine, radiating throughout your body, filling you with energy. You can balance the two energies, if you wish, by drawing on extra energy from the earth for more strength and power or from the universe for more lightness and expansion as you wish.

Keep this energy running up and down your spine and throughout your body until you feel filled and charged with energy.

Now, direct this energy toward doing the project. You will feel very motivated and excited (even if you didn't feel motivated before or were resisting or felt afraid to start this project). How you felt in the past no longer matters because you are now full of energy. You have the energy and enthusiasm to tackle the project. You feel confident. Even if you felt blocked before, your creative impulses are surging within you now, and you know you are able and ready to perform this task.

Now, as you direct this energy, see it flowing out of you as needed. Whatever you are going to do, see the energy coursing through you as needed, so you can direct it to that purpose. For example, if you want to write or type something, visualize the energy surging out through your hands. If you are going to lift heavy objects, visualize the energy coming out through your feet, body, and hands giving you extra strength. Return to the room and open your eyes, feeling charged with this energy.

Once you have finished this exercise, plunge immediately into your project. You'll have lots of energy and enthusiasm.

■The Healing Power of Sleep

While these energy-raising techniques are all designed to increase your energy level and can give you an added boost when you feel tired, they are not designed to replace needed sleep. Occasionally, though, we all miss some sleep, and then an energy-raising technique can fill the bill. If you find you are frequently tired or that you drift off while doing something, you obviously need more sleep.

CHAPTER 5

EMPOWER YOUR MIND
Achieve Your Goals

*M*any people don't get what they want because they don't believe in themselves enough; they don't believe they can get what they want. In turn, they don't want anything enough to try and get it. They may set a goal, but only half-heartedly work toward it, so the outcome is usually a half-hearted result, the wrong result, or no result at all. A good example of this is the person who says he or she wants to lose weight, but continually stops trying, regains weight, then resumes the diet, only to succumb to temptation and start to eat the wrong things again. Others set no goals at all and remain stuck in situations they don't really like. A classic example of this type is the person who hates his town or job but doesn't move, afraid to try something new.

By contrast, the person with a clear goal and a commitment to it can overcome all sorts of obstacles to achieve it. A good case in point is the heart-warming story of the Stolpas, a family who got trapped in a Nevada blizzard. Stolpa, his wife, and their baby could easily have died in the snow during their nine-day ordeal. His powerful determination and his belief that he could do it kept

James going for about thirty hours with almost no sleep as he trekked through about fifty miles of high snow drifts to find help.

When you recognize your inner power, you suddenly gain confidence and are motivated to go after and get what you want.

■How to Overcome Fear and Change Your Life

Anyone can make this transformation, even those who have been stuck in negative thinking for most of their lives. Even when things seem very grim and hopeless, those with an empowered mind can break through all sorts of blocks.

How Harriet Overcame a Health Crisis and Transformed Her Life

Harriet discovered this when she encountered a crisis in her own life. She was an independent long-widowed woman in her early sixties. She had retired from an administrative position and enjoyed the freedom of not having to work. She frequently got together with relatives and friends, enjoyed shopping, tended a collection of exotic plants, and though she lived alone, she was never really lonely.

But then she fell and fractured her hip. When she returned from the hospital with a large cast on her lower body, she had to hire people to care for her. The doctor explained she would be in a cast for about six weeks; then she could return to her normal routine.

Most people would accept the situation, make the best of it, and, after a few weeks, go back to their normal life. But Harriet turned the incident into a three-year disaster. Instead of focusing on what she really wanted—to get better and strengthen her ability to do so—she let her fear that she wouldn't succeed overwhelm her.

As a result, Harriet undermined her own power and was soon actively creating the problems she feared. Her hip took longer to heal than expected; she came to fear being alone but soon alienated her friends and relatives by rejecting their help and criticizing what they did.

Soon she was extremely depressed, and, unaware of her own role in creating these problems, she began dwelling more and more on her lack of ability to do anything. As she had less and less contact with others, she directed her anger inward. When relatives and doctors tried to help her, she resisted their help, insisting her situation was hopeless, no one could understand what she was experiencing, and no one could help. Harriet lost all confidence in herself, and she didn't realize the underlying problem was her own negative attitude.

Then, almost miraculously, when she reached her lowest point, everything turned around. She let her defeatist attitude go. It's hard to know exactly what triggered the change, except that Harriet literally faced death if she didn't. Looking back, Harriet feels this caused her sudden reversal. It took a crisis for her to realize that only the power of her own will could change her circumstances. She was then able to tap her own inner power. Finally, she pulled herself together, called the hospital, joined a group program, and began to look at what she could do to help herself.

Within a few weeks, the transformation was dramatic. She began calling her friends and relatives telling them she felt great. Suddenly she felt she could do anything. She had been to the very bottom and had pulled herself out. Now she wanted to pass on this message. She had done it; she now believed in herself. From feeling weak and helpless, she suddenly realized she could take back her personal power. She had only to reach out and do this, and it would be there. By believing this power was there, she could make it hers.

Underlying this transformation was a changed belief in herself. In thinking all was hopeless, Harriet lost faith in her own ability to help herself, and so she couldn't help herself. Her actions reinforced her beliefs, so she continued to feel helpless, friendless, and alone. But once her attitude changed, she realized she had to help herself, she came to believe she could do it, and she found she could. Now her actions affirmed life and strengthened her inner confidence. They became channels to empower her even further. For example, she reached out to others, so she no longer felt alone. She regained a sense of purpose and direction in life through helping others, which, in turn, helped her realize how much she could do. By helping others, by seeing that she mattered, she empowered herself.

The Circle of Empowerment Yields Positive Results

The interplay between Harriet's own empowering beliefs, which triggered her empowering actions, and the success of these actions that, in turn, reinforced her beliefs, continuously reinforce one another. To picture this interaction graphically, there is a circle of interaction and reinforcement that looks like this:

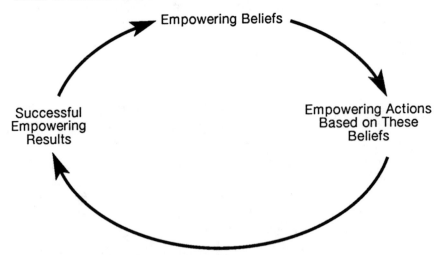

As you can see, if you believe in yourself and trust in your power to produce the results you want, you will create the experiences to support that belief. For example, if we believe we are attractive and people are attracted to us, we will exude that aura of confidence and act as if we expect their interest, so people will be drawn to us. If we are convinced we should have a certain job or promotion, we will express a feeling of assurance and act as if we belong in that job, so fellow workers and employers will think of us in that role.

■Believe in Yourself and Empower Yourself

Instead of giving in to fears and feelings of "I can't," turn those fears and feelings around, and say "I can." How? To overcome your fear and the "I can't" feeling, try acting as if you really can. When you act as if you believe you can, you actually empower yourself to do the thing you fear. That's because when you act as if you believe in yourself that action helps turn your belief into reality. Even if you don't really believe it at first, nurture that belief so it grows by taking on new tasks and responsibilities. You have it within yourself to do what it takes to reach your desired goals.

It all comes down to believing in yourself—and doing what you have to to create and sustain that belief. *You must believe and trust in your own power. If, at first, you don't believe it, create that belief by acting as if you do.*

Say "I Can" and Gain the Support of Others

Saying "I can" is a powerful way to gain the support and skills of others, who are attracted to working with a person with a can-do attitude. Such support, in turn, works to further expand what you can accomplish. Jim, for example, was heading a task force looking into making changes in the organization for which he worked. At first, he felt threatened when Paul, an expert in communications, approached him about joining his task force and made some suggestions about ideas for communications training. For a moment, Jim felt threatened by Paul. Jim had been researching ideas for change by asking people how they felt about the organization and what they thought needed change. Jim was a real pro when it came to research. He felt confident about what he was doing. But the communications training was new to him. Nevertheless, he realized that Paul's expertise would not only be good for the organization, but that he could learn something as well. He invited Paul to present his communications workshop, and, as a result, was praised for his vision and leadership in introducing a new program. By overcoming his fear of competition and maintaining the "I can" spirit himself, Jim gained new knowledge and skills that were useful both to him and to the organization. In turn, by mobilizing the skills of others, his leadership potential was recognized.

Jim succeeded because he confronted his fears head on. He didn't back down. Instead, putting his fears aside, he acted *as if* he weren't afraid of Paul's competition. At first, he didn't fully believe it; but he went past it, and acted *as if* he were unafraid. And, it worked! By empowering himself he gained the support of others and recognition from his company.

Focus on Your Good Qualities and Empower Yourself

This approach works because the action reinforces the belief. If you believe something, it will lead you to act to support that belief and, if that belief is correct, the result will reinforce the belief. For example, if you believe you can give a speech on a certain topic to a group and you have the necessary information, you will usually be able to give the speech successfully. That, in turn, will reinforce your belief in your ability to give good speeches. That's because actions that simulate being based on a belief can often produce the same successful results as actions based on a belief. Then, that successful outcome helps to create and reinforce the belief, as illustrated in the diagram below.

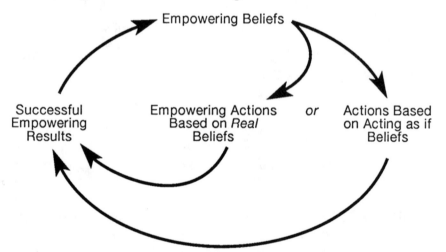

Empowering Beliefs

Successful Empowering Results

Empowering Actions Based on *Real* Beliefs

or

Actions Based on Acting as if Beliefs

By contrast, if you don't believe you can do something, you may act hesitantly, reflecting your lack of certainty. If that is the case, you may need to create some reinforcing experiences to help you overcome that uncertainty. Think of the popular claim, "If you believe you are great, you are great. . . . If you believe you can do it, you can." But what if you aren't really sure? How can you create the supporting experiences you need? How can you *act as if* you truly believed. How can you put aside your feelings of uncertainty and create the experiences that will support that belief?

One way to push past your fears—to take an action you want, affirm a belief in yourself, or have a greater sense of power generally—is to focus on your good qualities.

Often we feel uncertain about our ability to do something; we feel unsure of ourselves; we lack self-confidence. By focusing on what we can do, by reminding ourselves we were able to do certain things, we find we can do them.

For example, Nancy, a dental assistant, felt bored and un-fulfilled. She dreamed of starting her own jewelry design business but was afraid to leave her secure position and, instead, focused on the barriers to her goal, such as her limited funds and expe-rience. But underneath these concerns was her fear that she didn't have the ability.

For several years, she continued to work as a dental assistant. Then, at a workshop, one weekend, she learned to imagine what she wanted and saw herself pushing aside all the barriers. In her imagination, there were no "I can'ts"; no fears standing in her way. Instead, she focused on the qualities and abilities she had that could help her achieve her goal, and she thought about how she could put these into practice.

She listed these qualities in her mind and wrote them down: a good sense of design, a knowledge of what people like, persis-tence, a strong commitment to complete things once I choose to do them, a good ability to organize and direct people, and so on. Then, with these qualities in mind, she began imagining the steps she would need to take to start a business: hire a part-time assistant to sell her jewelry to stores and wholesalers; turn a room in her house into an office and workshop; create a letterhead and some flyers, and so on. As she visualized these possibilities, she realized she could start part time; then, once she built up the business, she could quit her job and do it full time.

Focusing on what she had and could do gave her the confi-dence she needed to start the process, and she began working toward her real desire. Empowered by this changed focus, she developed and put a series of action steps into practice. This made her feel even more confident that she could achieve her goal.

Like Nancy, you can focus on what you want and on the steps you need to take to achieve your desire. Begin by focusing on the skills and abilities you have that can help you reach that goal. Push away the "I can'ts"—thoughts about skills and abilities you don't have. Remind yourself you can always learn those skills, or you can find someone who has them, or you may find they may not be that necessary. See those barriers falling away.

Next, write down all the qualities and abilities you bring to what you want to do and think about the steps you must take to make it happen. Use the brainstorming technique (see Chapter 3) to come up with ideas. Write them down, rate them, set priorities and a time line indicating what you need to do and when. As you proceed, continue to remind yourself you can achieve your goal because you have all the qualities and abilities you need (or know where to find them).

Exercise 11 _____

RECOGNIZING YOUR GOOD QUALITIES AND USING THEM
TO ACHIEVE YOUR GOAL

(Time: 7–15 minutes)

The following exercise will help you build your feelings of empowerment. The goal is to concentrate on the positive things you bring to any situation. This helps reinforce your belief in yourself and your desire to reach your goal. The exercise will help you see yourself achieving your goal. The process is a little like building the foundation of a house and solidifying the structure. You need to shore it up with various supports, including:

1. your good qualities;
2. your desire to do something;
3. your belief that you can do it;
4. your vision of doing what you want to do.

_____

Each of these four elements helps to support the structure— the goal you want to achieve. Eliminate or weaken any of these elements and you weaken the structure—and your ability to achieve your goal.

The focus on your good qualities is the bedrock; it helps to strengthen and shore up the rest.

The following exercise will help you to become more aware of, acknowledge, and embrace your good qualities (personality traits, talents, and accomplishments, and so forth). Do this exercise whenever you are faced with a difficult task, new responsibilities, or a conflict or problem.

To prepare, copy the chart on page 69. The first part of the exercise is designed to build your sense of personal power by focusing on your good qualities; the second part will help you apply selected qualities to specific goals.

Start by closing your eyes and getting relaxed. Concentrate on your breathing for a minute or two to calm down.

Now, ask yourself each of the following questions and listen receptively to whatever comes:

"What are the personality traits I am most proud of?"

"What are the talents I am most proud of?"

"What are the accomplishments I am most proud of?"

Then, quickly write down whatever comes to mind. Keep going until you have at least ten traits, talents, and accomplishments listed. If you slow down or can't think of anything, ask the question again. Remain focused and concentrate on all your good qualities, all the good things you have done.

Next, review your list. As you read each item, create a mental picture of yourself with that quality, talent, or accomplishment. See yourself, experience yourself having that quality, using that talent, achieving that accomplishment. Let yourself feel good as you do so.

Then, think about your current goal or the problem you want to resolve. Remind yourself that you can do it because you have all these qualities and talents and accomplishments.

Now, imagine this desired goal or problem on a big white screen in front of you and ask yourself this question: "What qualities or talents do I have that I can use to help me achieve this goal/resolve this problem?" Let the answers just come to you; write down whatever comes. These may be qualities or talents you have already listed, or they may be new ones. Finally, imagine yourself achieving your goal or resolving your problem. See the goal attained or the problem resolved. Praise yourself and feel good about achieving or resolving it. (You may want to see yourself receiving some award or reward for what you have done.) Remind yourself that you have been able to do this because of all your good qualities, talents, and accomplishments. Finally, return to the room feeling very, very good for all you have, all you have done, and all you can do in the future.

■Focus on the Qualities You Want to Develop and Empower Yourself

In addition to focusing on the qualities you already have, you can feel more power by imagining you already have the qualities you want to develop and, by doing so, experience having those qualities. This means imagining that you already have those personality traits, talents, or abilities you want and that you have already achieved those future goals. In effect, you are using the affirmation process to tell yourself you have the qualities you want to develop; and you then go beyond simple affirmations to concentrate and focus your energy on experiencing these desired qualities. This imaginative process helps to turn these desires into beliefs that then get turned into action.

Affirmations work. By focusing on the qualities you want to achieve, you begin to feel you have these qualities. By changing your attitude about yourself, you change your actions to match your attitude. You begin to trust that you could be the way you want to be and that, as you act this way, others perceive and respond to you differently. By using this technique you can change your own feelings about yourself, the way you act, and the way others act toward you.

Remember the circle of empowerment (see page 64). In effect, by using affirmations, you are inserting another step at the beginning

MY GOOD QUALITIES

1. What are the qualities I am most proud of?

Personality Traits	Talents	Accomplishments
1.		
2.		
3.		
4.		
5.		
6.		
7.		
8.		
9.		
10.		

2. What qualities or talents do I have that will help me to achieve my goal or resolve my problem? How can they help me do so?

of the process—previsualizing what you want to be and turning what you envision into belief (see the illustration below).

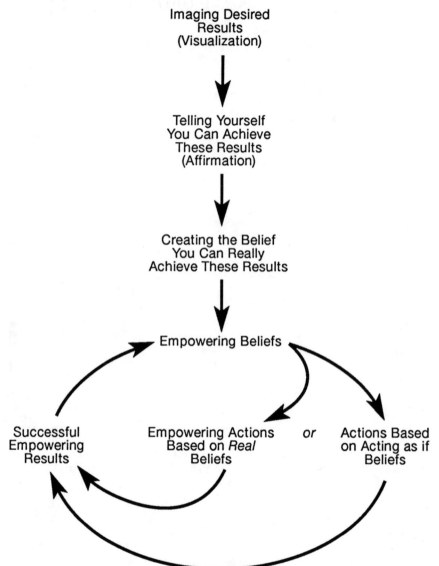

As this visualization process creates that belief, you feel more confidence because you believe in yourself. Thus, by affirming that you have what you want with the intensity of focus that creates belief, you can help overcome the fears and barriers standing in your way and make what you want happen.

You can use the following exercise to help you do this:

Exercise 12 _____

AFFIRMING YOUR BELIEFS ABOUT YOURSELF
AND YOUR FUTURE GOALS

(Time: 5–10 minutes)

To prepare, copy the chart on page 73 so you can write down the qualities you want to develop and the goals you want to achieve.

Start by closing your eyes and getting relaxed. Concentrate on your breathing for a minute or two to calm down.

Now ask yourself each of these questions and listen receptively to whatever comes:

"What are the qualities (traits, talents, or abilities) I most want to develop now?"

"What are the accomplishments I most want to achieve now? (or What is the problem I most want to solve now?)"

Then, quickly write down the first few qualities and accomplishments that come to mind. List about four or five of each. Then, looking at this list, choose whatever is most important to you and write that as an affirmation of something you already have—as if you had that trait, talent, or ability or as if you had already accomplished the thing you want or had resolved the problem you want to resolve. It is important to make your affirmation in the present tense, even though you don't really have that thing or quality because we create beliefs based on how we see ourselves, and those beliefs turn into actions and realities.

After you finish writing the affirmation, focus on it for about one to two minutes. Close your eyes, and repeat your affirmation over and over to yourself. As you do, see it and feel it happening. Imagine it is a movie you are in: You are playing the part. It is unrolling on the screen before your eyes. As you experience it, imagine you are sending all your concentrated energy to the image on your mental screen. Energize it; make it happen—turn up the volume, make the picture even more intense, maybe add surround sound or smells—make the experience vital and alive.

Finally, release the experience and return to the present, knowing that you are turning that experience into a true belief and making it happen.

You will need to repeat your affirmations over a period of time to reinforce them and make them truly real for you. Then you will be able to put them into practice. Plan to do this exercise daily for about a week for each affirmation you work with while you are trying to develop a new quality, accomplish something, or resolve a problem. As you do, you'll notice that the affirmation becomes more and more a part of you, and as it does, you will feel a greater sense of confidence and empowerment as you turn what you want to be or have into what is.

∎How to Overcome Past Failures

Even if you have experienced failures, you can put those aside and move on. The key is to regard any failure as an opportunity for learning and a stepping-stone to future success, so you don't remain stuck in the image of having failed. Remember, the failure is not you. You may have "failed" at doing something; but that is just one experience or one event in your life, not the only experience or event. It does not define who you are. *You* are not a "failure" because you have experienced a "failure." Tell yourself that and think about how you can learn from that experience to change something you do in the future to be more successful and move on.

Ann had difficulty developing relationships with men. She had long had a poor self-image. She dressed in a subdued, dowdy way and had recently put on about thirty extra pounds. In an image workshop, after focusing on her good qualities, she decided to make a change. She had tried before without success. As she thought about what had gone wrong before, she realized she had developed her poor self-image because she didn't like her looks and had reinforced this belief by gaining weight and dressing in a way that made her look even worse. Realizing that, she recognized that her first step was to focus on improving her appearance—to

IMAGINING WHAT I WANT TO BELIEVE ABOUT MYSELF

1. What are the qualities I want to develop or accomplishments I most want to achieve?

Personality Traits	Talents	Accomplishments
1.		
2.		
3.		
4.		
5.		
6.		
7.		
8.		
9.		
10.		

2. Affirmations: How it feels to have this quality or achieve this goal now:

a._____

b._____

c._____

lose weight. Next, she spiffed up her wardrobe with a more dynamic, colorful look. She even changed her hairstyle and make-up.

As she made these changes, her feelings of failure faded further and further into the past. It was as if she had become a new person and had left the failures behind with her old self. She was now ready to work on building a relationship.

If you, too, have felt like a failure, don't stay in that rut. You can put that failure behind you by following these steps:

1. Take some time to think about what happened to cause the failure and then think about how you can change the situation or yourself.

2. Be specific about what you need to change. If, for example, you feel it is something you did, ask yourself what exactly it was.

3. Select no more than two or three things to change at any one time. Make these changes before going on to make any others.

4. As you make each change, imagine your experience or experiences of failure as going back further and further in the past and being further and further away from you. Experience yourself becoming a new you.

∎Empower Yourself by Seeing Your Goal Achieved

Another way to feel a burst of self-power and confidence is by focusing on the resolution you want—whether this is a goal achieved or a problem resolved. If you visualize yourself as a person who has successfully attained a desired objective, it will reinforce the belief you want to hold. By imagining that you have already realized your goal, you feel more confident, more powerful, more dynamic, more directed—all feelings that add to your self-esteem and sense of empowerment.

In other words, by using mental imagery, you change your beliefs. You convince yourself that you already are experiencing what you want and have overcome any barriers to it. Your feelings and actions then respond to complement and reinforce that mental image.

This can be graphically illustrated on the circle of empowerment diagram previously described. In effect, you are adding an extra dose of energy and power through this imaging process. The circle of empowerment now looks like this:

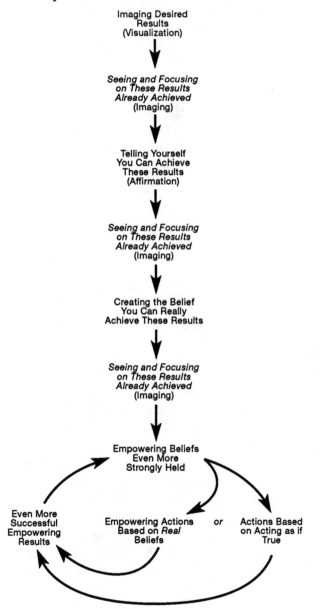

I have spoken with many people who did this successfully. After experiencing some difficulty—a broken relationship, a job they hated, a car they wanted but couldn't afford, a general lack of purpose and direction—they focused on and visualized themselves experiencing the success they wanted and subsequently reported a transformation in their lives.

The following exercise will help you do this yourself. Just put aside any feelings of uncertainty, fears you can't get it, worries about any obstacles that might stand in the way and concentrate on having what you want right now and believing you can have it and deserve it. Repeat this regularly for several days, perhaps along with the other exercises described in this chapter, to reinforce your objective, your belief in achieving it, and your confidence that you can do it.

Exercise 13

EXPERIENCING YOUR GOAL ACHIEVED

(Time: 3–5 minutes)

Begin by closing your eyes and getting relaxed. Take a minute or two to focus on your breathing until you feel calm and relaxed.

Now, imagine there is a large empty screen in front of you—and in a moment you see revealed on it an image of the way you want things to be. You see yourself having achieved your goal or having resolved your problem.

Whatever it is, it's happening right now and you are experiencing it fully. As you see it happening, put yourself in the picture. You are acting, interacting with others. Notice what's occurring. What do you hear? How do you feel?

Meanwhile, as you intensely experience all this happening, notice how good you feel about achieving your goal. You feel very satisfied, very powerful. You feel excited, energized, very strong, very self-confident. You feel fully in charge.

Now, notice others coming up to you or calling to congratulate you. They praise you for your success, and you feel warm and glowing as you receive praise. They tell you how proud they are of you for what you have accomplished. You feel wonderful, full of power, able to do anything you want in the future.

Take a minute or so to bask in this feeling of accomplishment and to reexperience attaining your desired goal. Then, when you feel ready, let this picture go and return to the room and everyday consciousness.

The exercises in this chapter can be used singly or together to help you feel greater confidence, self-esteem, and empowerment so you feel better about yourself and are better able to achieve your goals. They work by adding a charge of energy and focused attention. By repeatedly visualizing and affirming what you want and projecting your will and firm conviction that the result you want has *already occurred*, you begin to act in ways that further reinforce your beliefs. That conviction, in turn, leads to further actions based on these beliefs and so on around the circle of empowerment, where beliefs lead to actions that reinforce beliefs. Thus, by imagining changed actions, results, or beliefs, you can actually affect the outcome of events.

CHAPTER 6

BRING OUT YOUR BEST
Turn "I Can't" into "I Can"

*R*ecognizing and channeling your inner power is key to becoming the best you can be at something. Athletes, chess champions, and other competitors who succeed not only start with an inner talent or predisposition and work hard to make it happen, but they have a powerful belief in themselves and the motivation to focus that belief into a superior performance. Sometimes this churning desire to achieve is referred to as the "fire in the belly"—the gut-level drive that inspires one to go the distance. But beneath this fire is that burning mental desire or drive; that inner passion to do it that, combined with the belief that "I can and will," fuels action.

This drive can break through the various barriers that may stand in the way of achievement and can help us uncover those hidden skills and talents that might otherwise lie dormant.

The process is a little like a fighter bomber that flies its way through flak and enemy fire to achieve its objective. The flak is the personal "I can'ts"; the enemy fire is the external obstacles that slow us down or stop us along the way. But like the fighter bomber, if you press on, skillfully avoiding the flak and the fire, driven by the fuel that is your inner desire, and with the focus on the target that represents your will, then you can do it.

The trajectory of success in bringing out your best looks something like this:

I Can'ts

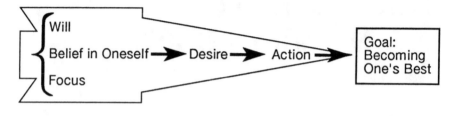

External Obstacles

So to realize your goal, you need to keep that desire channeled into action. At the same time you must maintain a belief in yourself, have the will to do it, and keep your focus on the goal. The "I can'ts" and the external obstacles must be dodged or kept out of the way.

∎Turning "I Can't" Messages into "I Can" Actions

"I can't" messages are among the biggest obstacles to becoming your best or to overcoming the everyday problems you encounter. But if everyday problems, obstacles, and challenges are turned into opportunities for learning and growth—the "I can" approach—they are positive experiences. "I can't" messages block the way and confirm themselves. Think you can't do it, and probably you can't. Think you can, and you probably can.

"I can't" messages frequently start in our childhood. Parents often convey these messages because they want to protect their child. Afraid the child can't meet the challenge and will be hurt or feel put down in trying, they fear letting him or her try. They say "no" and urge the child to do something else or "You can't," "You're not old enough," or the like. While such messages are necessary in some instances to keep children from real dangers, a knee-jerk "no" contributes to "I can't" thinking.

If a child hears these "I can't" messages often enough, they become internalized, and they block out potentially valuable learning experiences. Later, they can hold a person back from doing something he or she really wants, because the person thinks "I can't," when he or she really could do it by letting go of that message.

When I was a child, I found myself fighting back against such "I can't" messages from my parents, and when I found "I could" after all, I gained the confidence to fight against other "I can't" messages that came my way. One of my earliest experiences of this occurred when I was about seven or eight years old, in summer camp. My parents had signed me up for horseback riding lessons, and along with several other children, I had trouble learning to ride. We fell off a few times, and after a couple of potentially dangerous falls, the counselors decided we shouldn't take any more lessons. That may have been a good, safe decision.

But I was determined to learn to ride. A few days later, I sneaked back into the class. No one noticed, and this time I was so determined to stay on the horse that I did. By the time the counselors discovered me, I had proved I could do it and they let me stay in the class. Because I didn't let their "I can't" messages stop me and discovered I could, I grew more confident about trying other activities.

As I grew up, I found this experience of overcoming the "I can'ts" and discovering "I coulds" helped set the stage for future encounters. My parents, particularly my mother, kept saying "You can't"—do well in this course, handle this difficult job, succeed in this new place, and so on—but, having the will and the fire to do it, I did these things anyway. I was eager to try new things; I wanted to overcome, not shrink back from the challenges; and I accomplished them.

From "I Can't" to "I Can and Will"

By contrast, I have met many people who have been held back by "I can't" thinking, so they do or become much less than they could. Afraid to try and fail, they don't try, even though they probably could succeed if they did. Some are held back by the fear of not being perfect—if they can't be the absolute best very quickly, they feel there's no point doing something at all. By setting impossible standards for themselves, they don't try and don't fail. But they miss the point: The goal is not to be the absolute best in something, but to *be your own best*, to do and be the best you possibly can at what you want to do. What gives the feeling of exhilaration and empowerment is maximizing personal expression and attainment, not struggling to meet some abstract, impersonal standard set by someone else.

By confronting the "I can't" thinking, very often you find you can. Doing so can sometimes be very scary. You have to give up a comfortable habit. It also takes repeated practice to change what you are used to doing and feeling, but after awhile, by working on reprogramming your attitude and forcing yourself to do what you want but fear you can't, you will find you can do it. Moreover, when you do this in one area of your life, this "I can" approach will carry over into other areas as well.

I experienced this myself. When I was growing up, I was terrified of speaking in public, and I didn't say much when I was with others. I was afraid that what I wanted to say wasn't important and that nobody would want to listen. I was also afraid that people would think that what I said was stupid. I feared I might not remember what I wanted to say. As a result, when I did say anything, I spoke very fast, to get out my ideas quickly, so the listener wouldn't become impatient and tune me out.

Eventually, I desperately wanted to get over this fear. I saw it as a real barrier to doing what I wanted to do. So I began by forcing myself to speak whenever I could, as scary as that was. In high school and college, I volunteered to answer questions, and I often stumbled. But I kept doing it, and soon it became easier and easier. Then, after college, to learn to speak in front of a group, I joined Toastmasters, where I practiced both speaking extemporaneously and giving organized talks. To help me, I began visualizing myself in the role I wanted to assume—that of the comfortable, self-assured, interesting speaker.

Later, as a teaching assistant in graduate school, I applied what I had learned. At first, each time I stepped in front of the class, I feared that I might forget everything. But then I pushed past the fear to act the role, and within a few minutes the fears were gone and I was playing the role I imagined for myself. Subsequently, I used these same techniques to apply for and get a job as an assistant professor; and soon I was able to do workshops, seminars, and speak on the radio and television, too. By taking on each challenge in this "can do" spirit, I ended up with my own radio program and numerous guest spots on radio and TV.

In short, by getting rid of the "I can'ts," focusing intensely on the "I cans" through visualizing myself doing what I wanted to do, and practicing actually doing it despite my fear of doing so, I was able to push aside the barriers and get what I wanted.

And I have met many others who have turned their can'ts into cans. The key to achieving their goal was this attitude change— this "can do" belief that motivated them to stick to whatever they were doing and to achieve.

Eliminate the Critical; Accentuate the Supportive

An "I can" approach can be reinforced by not letting the negative thinking or critical judgments of others get you down and by not engaging in the "What will others think?" syndrome. Comparing yourself to others and thinking "I can't be as good" is just another way to pull yourself down. Of course, most of us can't succeed if we try to achieve professional standards without the necessary training or try to measure ourselves against someone with years of practice when we're just beginning. You're you and you have your own special combination of talents, skills, and interests. But then you may need additional training to accomplish certain tasks. If you don't get this training, or if you do but set unrealistic standards for yourself, you're just setting yourself up to fail and reinforcing your belief that you "can't." Certainly, select a successful role model, someone to serve as an inspiration to learn from and follow as a guide, but then think of what you can do as you.

For example, Peter got trapped in the cycle of comparing himself to others, failing, and concluding "I can't." He had not been able to succeed at what he really wanted because he was so afraid he couldn't measure up to the artists he especially admired. Though he was an excellent artist and photographer, he was afraid to enter competitions or to take his work around to the galleries; he couldn't face the prospect of being turned down. He remained stuck in routine jobs instead of pursuing more demanding and lucrative opportunities. He expressed his frustration by bad-mouthing many of the artists who got ahead, but never recognized how his own "can't do it" thinking that came from comparing himself to others stalled his career and fueled his bitterness.

Turning Your "I Can'ts" into "I Cans"

The following exercises and techniques are designed to empower you to change your "I can't" messages into "I cans."

They will help you to:

1. Recognize the "I can'ts" that are holding you back.
2. Decide which ones you want to eliminate first.
3. Decide what you can do to change them into "I cans."
4. Track your progress in eliminating the "I can'ts."
5. Make "I can" thinking a regular part of your life.

Exercise 14

DISCOVERING YOUR "I CAN'TS" AND IMAGINING "I CANS"

(Time: 7–15 minutes)

To get rid of the "I can'ts," you have be aware of them and decide which ones to get rid of first. This exercise will help you to gain this awareness and to decide your priorities for changing these "can'ts" into "cans."

Have a blank sheet of paper and a pencil ready or use the chart on page 86. Then, close your eyes and get relaxed.

Now, looking at your inner mental screen, ask yourself this question: "What do I think I *can't* do that I would like to do?" Then let your imagination go and notice what comes. As you discover each new "can't," write it down under the column headed: "What I Can't Do But Want to Do." Spend about 2 to 3 minutes listing your "can'ts."

Then ask yourself: "What would I like to do if I could?" Again, let your imagination go and write what comes in the appropriate column. You may find some of the answers are the same, but you may find new ones by phrasing the question in this way. Spend about 2 to 3 minutes doing this.

Now go back over your list and rate those "I can'ts" and "I would like tos" on a scale of 1 (top priority) to 5 (lowest priority) on how important it is to you to change these things. Now you can select the "I can'ts" you first want to work on overcoming.

Exercise 15

CHANGING "I CAN'TS" INTO "I CANS"

(Time: 5–10 minutes)

After identifying the "can'ts" you want to work on, the next step is deciding what you can do to change them into "cans." What resistances or fears are holding you back? What practical steps might you take to overcome any resistances? What might you do to prove you can? What actions should you take now?

You can use the chart on page 87 to help you do this.

Again, close your eyes and get relaxed. Then, focusing on the "I can't" you have selected to change into an "I can," ask the following questions. Let the answers come to you and write down the answers:

"What resistances or fears are holding me back? Why do I feel I can't do this?"

Then, after the answers have stopped coming, ask:

"Are there any other resistances or fears I may have? Is there anything I haven't noticed or don't want to notice?"

Again let the answers come and write them down.

Now that you have listed any resistances or fears, ask yourself what you might do to overcome them and change that "can't" into a "can." This time, see what ideas come to you when you are in a receptive

IDENTIFYING MY "I CAN'TS"

What I Can't Do But Want to Do	Rating (Scale 1–5)		What I Would Like to Do if I Could	Rating (Scale 1–5)

CHANGING MY "CAN'TS" INTO "CANS"

The "Can't" I want to change: _____ + ____

The "Can" I want to change it into: _____

The Resistances and Fears Holding Me Back	What I Can Do to Change the "Can't" into "Can" Now	Rating (Scale 1–5)

mode with your eyes closed. And then try brainstorming in a more active mode with your eyes open. Again, write down what you might do.

For example, say you have a fear of speaking. Your list of resistances and fears and your list of what you can do might look something like this:

Resistances and Fears:	What I Might Do:
Looking foolish	Join Toastmasters
Forgetting what I want to say	Volunteer to conduct interviews
Not being good enough	Practice in front of my mirror
Being embarrassed	Speak into my tape recorder
Being boring	Go door to door in a political campaign

Then, having identified the things you might do, go back over the list and rate them from 1 (top priority) to 5 (lowest priority) to show what you would most like to put into practice now. Then, within the next day or two, start doing that.

■Chart Your Progress

As you work on discovering and eliminating your "can'ts," it helps to chart your achievements along the way. It generally takes about three weeks to get rid of a habit, so figure it will take you about this long to change your "I can't" approach into an "I can" attitude.

Charting your achievements not only lets you know how you are doing, but it helps to set up milestones and shows points along the way at which you can reward yourself for your achievements. If, for example, you are working on losing weight, you may want to do something special to recognize your achievement every time you lose five pounds. If you are working on overcoming a fear, you might reward each breakthrough with a wonderful meal.

A regular datebook or daily calendar is fine for this purpose. Simply check off each day you have stayed on course or each time you achieved a particular objective. You may want to add comments to yourself, such as: "Good speech," or "Congratulations at resisting that cake at the office party."

∎Make "I Can" Thinking a Part of Your Life

Besides working on overcoming specific "I can'ts," you can work on stopping "I can't" thinking any time you encounter it. For example, when someone asks you to do something or when you are trying something new, do you find yourself saying "I can't"? If so, ask yourself why you are saying no. Is it because you really don't want to do the thing; is it because you truly can't for a legitimate reason (such as a conflict in time, a skill you can't acquire in time to do the job, and so forth), or is it because fear or resistance is preventing you from doing something you really would like to do. If it's the latter, try saying "Yes, I can," and do what you need to do to make it happen. If you make this a habit, you'll find you can do all sorts of interesting and enjoyable things you might otherwise have blocked yourself from experiencing.

"I can" thinking has carried me along many roads. It led to my setting up several sales organizations in multilevel marketing, which, in turn, led to my consulting and writing on the subject which further led to a published book on the topic and to many successful speaking engagements.

It would have been very easy to say, "No, I've never done this before," when I began doing this and later when I was invited to be the lead speaker and workshop leader at a 2-day conference for sales leaders, since I had never done either before. But, by pushing aside my initial "I can't" fears and simply saying, "Sure, I'll give it a try," I figured out how to do it, and I did it successfully. By focusing on *what to do* to make the "I can" happen, not on *whether* I could, and by acting the role I wanted to play, I became what I wanted to be. By believing "I can," I could. As I got to know others in the field, I realized that many of them had no previous experience either, but they, too, had become very successful, because they believed they could.

Whenever you face anything new or threatening, notice if you have a tendency to say, "I can't." It's often just a knee-jerk reaction to the idea of change. If that's your typical response, be aware and stop yourself before you say it. Ask yourself, is it that you really can't, or is it just a general attitude of resistance or fear that is holding you back? If that's the case, don't say "I can't" right away. Instead, say "I can" or "I'd like to consider it," and then, if you *can*—and want to—do this, say "I can." Once you say "I can," you'll find the way to make it happen. Saying it will help you believe it and, in turn, will help to make it happen. So say it!

MENTAL IMAGING

The Power to Maximize Your Skills and Abilities

*O*nce you get rid of the "I can'ts," you'll be free to develop your talents and skills. In all probability, you'll find you now can do many things you never dreamed were possible, and you can develop existing talents and skills to new levels of excellence.

Researchers, trainers, and creativity consultants now widely recognize the power of the mind to affect performance. Hundreds of consultants and trainers have been showing business leaders and their employees how to use these techniques to improve productivity and boost morale. Thousands of sports figures use mental imagery techniques to develop and perfect their skills and win competitions. They mentally practice their sport to supplement actual practice, and, before a big competition, they psych themselves up by visualizing themselves winning the game.

This technique is also used by professionals in many fields. After they prepare their written materials, many trial lawyers review in their mind exactly how they are going to present their argument in court. They visualize themselves speaking to the jury. They see themselves questioning and cross-examining witnesses. They go through all the different phases of the trial in their mind as the case moves on from day to day. Teachers, seminar leaders, salespeople, and others use this technique to develop and perfect their skills.

How Dan Used Visualization to Get the Job He Wanted

After Dan was laid off from a telemarketing job, he was uncertain what his next move should be. Using visualization techniques, he imagined himself in a variety of jobs. As he saw himself in different jobs, he became more and more aware that he really liked working with people—directly—not behind a phone bank, as he had in his last position. Given the best arena for his skills and background, he decided on direct out-in-the-field sales.

Now he needed to decide what to sell. He continued his visualizations. Since he was already a computer buff, he saw himself selling computer systems and software. He imagined how he would sell these products. In preparing for an interview, he visualized himself selling that company's product line, and, with this preparation, he was able to do a series of mock sales presentations for the interviews. He had mentally organized everything he would say and do in the actual presentation. If, as he visualized, he made a mistake or didn't have just the right tone or level of enthusiasm, he would correct it in his mind and do it again the right way. By the time he had the interviews, he knew he was ready.

Visualization helped him feel fully prepared and full of confidence for the real thing. The result was a very compelling pitch, and a few days later he was hired. He had never done one-on-one direct selling before; but because he recognized and practiced what he needed to do in his mind, he was able to develop the professional polish needed for the job—and he convinced his prospective employer that he could do it.

■Mental Scripts: The Power to Plan and Rehearse

Mental imaging techniques work because they give you the ability to plan what you want to do and practice doing it. By doing so, you gain the confidence that comes from practice. If you can actually practice, so much the better. But even if you are just rehearsing in your mind, you are practicing, and your mind creates a mental script so real that when it comes time for the real thing, you can use your mental script as a guide.

I use these techniques regularly to prepare for talks and presentations. I mentally go through all the steps a few times to decide what materials I am going to use in a presentation and how I am going to use them. Then, I mentally rehearse the broad outlines of my talk, and if I need to make any changes or additions to what I say or how I say it, this practice gives me the chance to make them. By the time I actually give the talk, everything I need to do it well is in place, and I feel confident I can do it.

Like Dan and me, you can use visualization to build your skills. I begin by using a series of visualizations to ask myself what I need to do. Based on these insights, I start my preparations. If it's a seminar, for example, I create an outline and workbook, and then I imagine myself giving the talk. I see myself on the platform. Using the outline, I go through each topic in my mind, making appropriate changes and additions. When the time comes to give my talk, I am confident that I can do it. I know in my mind what I can do, and, when the seminar begins, I step out on the stage, and it's as if I had done it many times before. Once I start speaking, everything seems to fall right into place, just as I had imagined it. The ideas and words are right there when I need them, and I zip along following my outline. When it comes time for audience participation, the audience, too, slips right into place.

It all works, because I go over everything in advance in my mind's eye. As a result, I know what I am going to do and have the confidence to do it. The "I can" approach opens the door and the mental script technique helps you through it.

How Mental Rehearsal Works to Increase Your Skills

This technique works because, as you actively see yourself performing well, you reinforce what you have learned from physically performing that act or learning that skill. Since the mind doesn't distinguish between what you *really* do and what you do mentally, if you perform well mentally, the mind sets up an effective pattern (like a habit) which, in creating mental images that lay down traces in the brain cells, transfers over into the real performance. You see yourself performing something perfectly; that, in turn, provides an ideal model toward which you can strive when you are actually doing it.

Practicing in your mind also reduces the actual amount of practice time needed and, therefore, helps you improve more quickly. Then, too, as you visualize going through the experience, you learn what you need to add or change to improve your performance.

∎Seven Keys to an Award-Winning Mental Rehearsal

To use the mental rehearsal technique successfully, keep these key points in mind.

1. *See yourself performing perfectly.* Create an ideal model to guide your performance. Imagine doing whatever you are doing flawlessly and effectively. Remember, the image in your mind is what will gradually translate itself into reality. If you make mistakes in your mental practice, you'll make the same mistakes in the real world. If you imagine yourself performing perfectly— you'll perform perfectly—or at least more closely to perfection in the real world. Whatever skill you choose to develop, imagine you know just what to do. For example, to improve your typing skills, see yourself hitting every key correctly and quickly. To be a better speaker, see yourself making the perfect presentation. To be more comfortable and glib in relating to people, see yourself moving easily around a group at a party or business gathering.

2. *Quickly correct any mistakes.* If, as you visualize, you make a mistake, imagine yourself quickly correcting it. For example, if you are imagining a job interview and say the wrong thing, back up to what you were doing before you made the error and give your answer again. If you are making a presentation and don't like the way you moved or gestured, repeat the scene in your mind, moving and gesturing in a way you like.

3. *Find a good role model.* Even if you already have some experience with a skill you want to develop, a good role model can give you an ideal toward which to strive in your own mental practicing. If you can, observe the person in action. Then, imagine yourself in this person's place reenacting as closely as possible what this person did so well. For instance, if you have seen someone give an impressive speech, imagine yourself giving a talk using the same approach. If you have met someone who is especially adept in meeting and talking to people, pay attention to what he or she does; then mentally practice these methods.

4. *Make your imagination as intense and vivid as possible.* Make the image or experience as real as possible. The more real you make the mental experience, the more powerful it will be in influencing what happens when you actually do it. So don't just visualize yourself using the desired skills effectively, but hear, feel, smell, and otherwise sense the environment. Make whatever you see as detailed and real as possible: As you visualize the setting, notice what you and others are wearing. Pay attention to what others are doing; are they responding to you, are they listening closely and enjoying your comments?

5. *Invest the image with the feeling of becoming more skilled, confident, and assured.* You want to invest the image with these feelings, because they will stay with you when you return to normal consciousness and will help you perform better in real life. When you feel good about what you are doing, you enjoy doing it more and so you will do it better.

6. *Repeat your visualization again and again.* Like any athlete or performer giving a performance, you have to practice—in your mind, just as in life. So repeat your visualization at least two or three times, more if needed. By doing so, it becomes automatic, a habit. If necessary, you can replay this guiding imagery in your mind at any time.

7. *Avoid second-guessing yourself.* After you have successfully visualized what you want to do, let yourself feel a sense of completion. Don't question whether the process works, or ask, "Can I really do this?" Such questions will undermine what you have

done. You have to truly believe that mental imaging will work for it to do so. Should questions about the process arise, push them away. Keep reinforcing your self-confidence and assure yourself that you can do it. That, too, will help you do it.

▮How to Use Mental Imaging

The following visualization exercises will give you an idea of how to use this process. They can be adapted to the skill you want to acquire or improve.

Exercise 16

IMAGINING YOU POSSESS THE SKILL YOU WANT TO ACQUIRE

(Time: 5–10 minutes)

To begin, close your eyes and get relaxed. Focus on your breathing for a minute or two to calm down.

Now ask yourself what skill, talent, or ability you want to acquire. Let a word or picture of this skill come into your mind. Then picture someone performing that skill very well. It could be a person you know, maybe even someone well known; it could be anyone. Just watch the person in action.

Watch the person closely. He seems to be completely at ease. He is doing it very well. Notice how he moves. Notice his gestures. Notice that he feels very confident and assured. He has lots of enthusiasm. He really likes what he is doing and is totally into doing it. Maybe there are others watching him, too, and admiring what he is doing. Continue to watch for awhile, really getting a sense of what he is doing, so you see what to do yourself. . . .

Now, after you have watched for awhile, go over to the person you have been watching. Explain how much you have admired what he has done and ask him to be your teacher. Explain how much you really want to learn to do this yourself. Then, listen to the person's answers.

If the person says no, ask again. If the answer is still no, perhaps you aren't quite ready to learn this skill, or learn from this teacher. Ask why . . .

If the answer is yes, then see yourself getting ready to start learning this skill, and see your teacher nearby, watching, ready to help. Then, recalling how you saw your teacher do it, imagine yourself doing it. If you're not sure of something, you can always turn to your teacher to ask for help. Now spend a few minutes practicing this skill as your teacher watches. Notice how you move as you do it. Notice how you are feeling very confident and assured that you will do well. Also, you have lots of enthusiasm. You really like what you are doing, and feel totally absorbed. . . .

When you feel ready, stop practicing and thank your teacher for helping, knowing you can always call on him or her to help again. Then, let this image go, return to the room and open your eyes, feeling very good and confident in your new abilities.

Exercise 17

PRACTICING A SKILL OR TALENT YOU WANT TO DEVELOP

(Time: 3–5 minutes)

To begin, close your eyes and get relaxed. Focus on your breathing for a minute or two to calm down.

Ask yourself what skill, talent, or ability you want to further develop. Then see yourself ready to perform this skill, with whatever equipment you need to do this. If you wish, invite your teacher to come and observe and make comments and suggestions.

Now whatever the skill, see yourself doing it. Notice that you feel comfortable, very much at ease. Experience yourself performing this skill very well, and as you do, notice how you are moving. You are moving easily; you feel competent and confident. Should you make a mistake, you can quickly correct it, or if your teacher is there, ask your teacher what to do to correct it. Or you can turn and see someone near you practicing the same skill and doing it perfectly. You can copy what this person is doing, so you know exactly what to do. If you wish, you can have others around who are just watching; they are praising and cheering you.

Take a few minutes to continue to practice, doing it well, and feeling self-assured and powerful. You know you are very good and are getting even better as you practice.

Then, when you feel ready, finish practicing, and if you have had any help thank whoever has helped. If others have been watching, thank your fans for their support. Then let the image go, return to the room and open your eyes, feeling good and confident that you are getting better and better in your abilities.

∎Creating Your Own Visualizations

These exercises are just models you can use to develop new skills or practice others you want to further develop. Such skills and abilities can run the gamut—from job or hobby skills to social skills. You can insert whatever skill you want to develop into these scenarios, or you can create your own visualizations, anything from an elaborate setting in which to practice your skills to simply seeing yourself practicing in your mind's eye.

The idea is to decide what skill you want to develop, create a setting in which you are comfortably using that skill, and then see and experience yourself doing it perfectly. For the visualization to be most effective, make the image and experience as vivid and intense as possible, so it feels very real. It's important to notice any mistakes as you practice and correct them immediately, so you don't carry the errors over into your performance.

Practice regularly for a week or two. After you have practiced several times, you will begin seeing the results in your improved performance. Continue with the visualization until you have acquired the facility you want. Once you attain this level, if you actually perform this skill regularly, your everyday habit reflexes will take over and soon you'll be able to do it automatically and effectively.

Once you attain this automatic performance level, you will no longer need to regularly practice mentally. However, from time to time, polish your abilities by going over your skill in your mind. And if you expect to use the skill for a particularly critical occasion, mentally review, so you feel completely prepared and psyched up to perform at your best.

Should you attain a desired level and want to improve even more, simply bring up the image of your ideal accomplishment in your mind. For example, choose an even more skilled teacher as your model. Then practice to achieve that level. Just as in everyday life you want to keep improving, so likewise you need to improve the models you use to practice in your mind.

CHAPTER 8

RE-CREATE YOURSELF
How to Shape
Your Personality

*W*e are all constantly playing different roles in different situations and with different people. We are tough with some people, soft and gentle with others. We act like a little kid with some, like a nurturing parent with others, like an aggressive barracks sergeant with still others. We are all business with some people, wild and crazy with others. And often the situation shapes the role we play—from the business meeting to the office party to the Halloween or New Year's celebrations, when we step into different costumes to take on different roles.

But what about with new people and new situations? What if we have new roles to play and we aren't sure what to do? Or what if we aren't sure we can do it? Or suppose we aren't sure the particular role we have been playing will fly with a new boss or in a new company with a new group of people? There are many occasions when there is an uncertain fit between who we usually are or expect to be and the role required in a new and unfamiliar situation. Take some of these common examples:

➤ You are asked to take charge and aren't sure what to do.

➤ You have to make a career change because of changed economic circumstances, and the culture of the new field is very different from the one to which you were accustomed.

➤ You are working with a new group of people who have different values and expectations, and you want to get along.

➤ You want to advance to a new position where you have to take on different tasks and roles.

All such changes mean you must learn to act in a new way, perhaps change your image and bring out a hidden side of you.

It's also possible that you may want to change to be more like someone you admire. Or maybe you have a hidden side of yourself you want to express. Or perhaps, the way you have been acting isn't working. For example:

➤ You are too shy and unassertive to get what you want or to get ahead.

➤ You are often difficult to work with because you are too sensitive and irritable.

➤ You are too pushy and aggressive, so that people you would like to work with are often afraid of you or try to avoid you.

In short, for one reason or another you need to make some personality changes to alter the way you act or are, so you fit in better or get along better with people. It sounds difficult, but when you do change, the results will amaze you: a more satisfying job, one you really like; greater success in working with others; increased opportunities—all because you have learned to be more flexible.

How Sam Transformed Himself from Shy Techie to Confident Marketer

Sam had been fairly shy and bookish. He worked as a systems engineer in a high-technology field building rockets and space equipment. People looked up to him for his knowledge, and he was praised for his quiet persistence, conscientiousness, and precision. Outwardly, there was a good fit between Sam's work and the way he behaved.

However, Sam was unsure of himself with people; he felt ill at ease going to parties and making small talk. On his job this didn't matter; Sam's employers were more interested in his technical designs than how he interacted with others.

For several years, nothing changed. Sam imagined that it would be nice to be more outgoing and socially comfortable, but he did nothing about it since he was relatively comfortable in the niche he had created for himself.

But then, due to cutbacks, Sam suddenly found himself out of work in a market much less receptive to his skills. He *had* to change, not because he might like to be different, but for his own economic survival.

Sam began thinking about the kinds of jobs that were available and realized that he would need to improve his social skills if he were to land one of them. He decided to use his technical skills to market high-tech products and began to work on making himself over in order to step into this new role. At first, he was nervous about approaching people to sell them anything. But he began imagining himself in this role and practicing at home in front of his mirror. Finally, he gained enough confidence to start interviewing and landed a job in telemarketing. Later, as he gained more confidence from both his success on the phone and his mental visualization and mirror practice at home, he got a job as an outside rep. Gradually, he moved from *playing* the role of enthusiastic high-tech marketing rep to actually *being* the one.

At the same time, the new, more outgoing personality characteristics he adopted in his new work carried over into his personal life, and he found he was more comfortable in social situations. He had gradually left his shyness behind as he became accustomed to working with people. After awhile, he was no longer the shy bookish systems engineer he had been. He had become a knowledgeable and friendly high-tech marketing rep, and that felt good.

■How You Can Make a 180 Degree Change in Your Personality

Sam's dramatic change—from shy introvert to outgoing extrovert—illustrates that you can change even your most basic personality traits when necessary. Although we develop certain traits as a result of our own experiences—and certain traits may feel more comfortable to us, making us think something is "our nature"—we are, in fact, very plastic and can adapt in many ways. Even what may at first seem like a 180 degree transformation may come to seem very natural, and after awhile, we may be able to shift back and forth between styles, choosing whichever style is more appropriate to a particular situation. Or the new trait may virtually replace the older one if we have made permanent changes in our lives.

The key is to determine the personality traits that no longer work and figure out what qualities you need to adopt to be successful. Then, you can work on practicing these new traits. If, like Sam, you have to learn to be more outgoing and comfortable with people, you would do things such as:

➤ put yourself in social situations, such as parties and professional mixers, and force yourself to meet and talk to people;

➤ volunteer to do things in a social organization that force you to relate to people, such as helping to set up programs and introduce speakers, hosting meetings, or doing publicity for the group;

Alternatively, if you want to become more introspective and thoughtful, you would put yourself in such situations such as:

➤ going on a weekend retreat to a place noted for its calm and peaceful location;

➤ volunteering to do library research for an organization.

Use the chart on page 103 to help you identify traits that are no longer working in your new situation, determine traits you need to adopt, and consider things you can do to help you become more comfortable with this new style.

PERSONALITY TRAITS: WHICH TO CHANGE AND HOW TO CHANGE THEM

New Situation Requiring Change	Differences in New Situation	Personality Traits that Aren't Working	Personality Traits I Need to Develop	What I Can Do to Develop These New Traits

■Creating Balance: Controlling the Different Aspects of Your Personality

Another way to create a change in your personality is to know when to use the traits you have. To do this, you need to be aware of when you are expressing different traits so you can use each of them more appropriately. It's not that the trait doesn't fit the situation and that you have to develop the opposite trait (as in Sam's case). Rather you need to be able to control the use of that trait that works in certain contexts and use a different trait in others. This allows you to respond at your best to the wide range of situations you confront in your daily life.

Paul was the coordinator of a large volunteer organization. The members really loved him because he was kind and caring. They also liked his casual spontaneity that helped people feel immediately at ease. At the same time, these traits sometimes led to problems. Paul had trouble managing the group—he was often too nice, spontaneous, and disorganized. Since he wanted so much to help people and be liked, he sometimes lacked the discipline necessary to control the group, and at one point he tried an experiment in democracy that led some members of the group to rebel and try to run the program themselves.

Paul's need was not to stop being nice, caring, and spontaneous, but to better control these traits and balance them with others—assertiveness, firmness, and discipline—that he could use when needed. After the attempted coup, Paul realized what he needed to do and began to alter his personality. He continued to express the warm, friendly, caring traits that endeared him to others, but he toned them down and worked at controlling them. He became more direct and forceful when necessary. As a result, he reestablished his authority, and the attempted coup ended. At the same time, realizing he needed help getting organized, he recruited some people who were better organized to help organize his office, and he set up a system to keep track of his papers and the tasks he needed to do.

∎Four Steps to Changing Your Personality

The four basic steps to personality change are:

1. Determine how you want to change—what or who do you want to become?
2. Create a mental script—imagine yourself in the new role.
3. Practice your mental script to reinforce your new image of yourself.
4. Play out your mental script in real life.

Start by asking yourself: "How would I like to change? What or who do I want to become?" What aspects of your personality don't you like? Imagine their opposite. For example, if you feel you are too quiet and retiring, think about what it would be like to be more assertive and outgoing. If you feel you are too stand-offish and reserved, imagine yourself participating more. If you lack confidence, see yourself as an assured, confident person.

In short, change the picture of yourself. Replace the qualities you don't want with a picture of yourself possessing the qualities you do.

Exercise 18 _____

CHANGING THE QUALITIES YOU DON'T WANT
INTO THOSE YOU DO

(Time: 5–10 minutes)

Copy the chart on page 106. In column one list those qualities you would like to change. List them as they occur to you; don't try to edit or analyze them. Then, in column two, list an opposite or different quality—the one you would like to replace it with. Write down the first quality that comes to mind so you keep your responses spontaneous. Finally, for each pair, create a picture in which you see yourself in a scene with the original quality. Again, let the picture come to you. Then imagine that this picture is suddenly being torn up; and see yourself

CHANGING YOUR PERSONALITY

Qualities I Don't Want	*Opposite or Different Qualities I Do Want*
1.	1.
2.	2.
3.	3.
4.	4.
5.	5.
6.	6.
7.	7.
8.	8.
9.	9.
10.	10.
11.	11.
12.	12.

with the opposite (or different) quality. Experience yourself possessing this quality for about a minute. Go through the list; select those changes that are most important to you and repeat the visualizations of yourself first with the old quality, then with the new. Repeat the visualization over the next few days and then try putting each one into practice.

■How to Shape Your Personality Type

Besides changing individual qualities, you can also work on changing your overall personality type. This is a more extensive transformation, but it is worth doing if you feel the way you are isn't working for you or that another way will work better for you. This may be especially needed if you've been thrust into a new situation; one that can't be changed and so necessitates that you change your-self—if, for example, you are shy and suddenly find yourself in the limelight, or you've been very active and now find yourself living a more quiet, isolated life. What is needed in such cases is personal-ity-type transformation to suit the change in circumstances.

You can create and direct this transformation by consciously choosing the personality style you want to adopt, and, if you have not been forced into this change by outside circumstances, you can also choose the setting.

Determining Your Personality Type

To change, you need to know what your overall personality type is now and what type you would prefer to be.

A good system for recognizing your type is the Myers-Briggs Type Indicator, which is used by many psychologists and human resources professionals. If you actually have an opportunity to take the Myers-Briggs test, which consists of about 100 multiple-choice questions, you can formally rate yourself and come up with a score to identify the different characteristics that distinguish the type of person you are.[1]

---

1 The Myers-Briggs Type Indicator was developed by Katharine C. Briggs and Isabel Briggs Myers. It was published originally in 1943 by the Consulting Psychologists Press, Palo Alto, California, and has been revised numerous times since. It is available in a variety of different forms, some of which have a different number of questions.

But even without a formal test, you can use your inner mental powers to arrive at a general sense of what your personality type is.

Your personality type is determined by your preferred way of relating to others and to the world—how you focus your attention, acquire information, make decisions, and orient yourself toward the outside world. There are two opposite types of preferences for each of these four categories, and, while we all use both types at different times, each of us has certain preferred models that we use more frequently and more confidently than others. Since you have both abilities at all times, you can alter your preferences and use the other mode with greater frequency or more confidence should you choose to do so.

The Myers-Briggs system distinguishes the four preferences as:

Extroversion Versus Introversion. If you tend to focus primarily on the outer world (people or things), you are extroverted; if you tend to focus on your inner world, you are introverted. Typically, extroverts prefer to communicate by talking rather than by writing; they like to experience the world to understand it, so they are drawn to action and variety. By contrast, introverts tend to like working quietly by themselves; they prefer to understand the world before experiencing it, so they tend to reflect before acting.[2]

Sensing Versus Intuition. If you tend to focus on the realities of a situation, you are considered a sensing person; if you tend to be more concerned with the meanings, relationships, and possibilities that go beyond what you learn from your senses, you are considered to be an intuitive person. These differences are reflected in everyday personality styles. Sensing people tend to be more here-and-now oriented; they are more realistic and practical; they are especially interested in facts, details, and working with established procedures. Those who are more intuitive tend to be less detail oriented and more interested in the overall

---

[2] Myers-Briggs Type Indicator Report Form, p. 2.

picture; they are especially interested in thinking about new possibilities, and they enjoy using their imagination.

Thinking Versus Feeling. If you tend to make decisions objectively, consider the facts and assess the evidence, you are considered a thinking type; if you are more apt to make decisions based on how you feel about something and how important it is to you or others, then you are a feeler. Thinkers tend to be analytical in the way they approach things; they consider the consequences of their choices and tend to analyze and evaluate things. Feelers tend to be warmer and more sympathetic when dealing with people; they are more concerned with harmony and relationships in making their choices than with objective standards.

Judging Versus Perceiving. If you like structure and organization in the way you relate to the outer world, you are a judging type; if you tend to be more flexible and spontaneous, you have a perceiving approach to life. Those drawn to judging tend to want to live a more regulated, controlled life, where things are planned and orderly. By contrast, perceivers tend to be very receptive to new information and are open to experience, ready to adapt to what occurs, rather than organizing and planning it in advance. Rather than trying to control things, they are more interested in understanding them.[3]

If the different orientations for each of these preferences are combined, the result is sixteen different possible ways to relate to oneself, other people, and the world.

These sixteen types can be grouped and combined into four subgroups, each composed of four types:

Introverted Sensing Types. This group tends to be very quiet, inward looking, and practical. While some are more thoughtful in the way they approach things, others tend to be more sensitive to others; still others tend to be judgmental and critical, while some are more flexible in the way they respond.

---

3 Myers-Briggs Type Indicator Report Form, pp. 2–3. These represent a rewrite of the Myers-Briggs descriptions of these types and a summary of these types as often presented by members of a society devoted to researching type based on the Myers-Briggs model—the Association for Psychological Type.

Introverted Intuitive Types. This group also tends to be quiet and inward looking but they are more original, even visionary in their approach. They tend to like ideas. While some are logical and organized in their approach, others are more informal.

Extroverted Sensing Types. This group tends to be very sociable, realistic, practical people. They get along well with others and tend to be good team players. While some are especially good at problem solving and organizing things, others are especially good at promoting harmonious relationships.

Extroverted Intuitive Types. This group tends to be very outgoing and assertive. They are responsive to others but are also good problem solvers and leaders. They tend to have lots of ideas, which they share with others. While some are especially good at coming up with ideas, others excel at relating to others and helping them resolve problems.

These capsule sketches provide a brief overview of one common way of categorizing different personality types. You can combine this system with the more intuitive, mental-imaging approach described in this book to determine your own type. First, look at each of these preferences individually and recognize the qualities you feel define you. Second, think about how well these traits have been working for you, and then determine if you want to further develop or change any of them.

Exercise 19

YOUR PERSONALITY TYPE; DECIDING WHAT TO CHANGE

(Time: 10–15 minutes for each part)

The first part is designed to help you think about your major personality characteristics, how well they are working for you, and whether you want to make any changes. The next part will help you work on making these changes. Copy the chart on page 111 to record your experiences. You can do this exercise in four separate segments for each of the pairs of characteristics, or do them sequentially.

Relax and close your eyes. Focus on your breathing going in and out, in and out for a minute or two until you feel very relaxed and calm.

CHARTING MY PERSONALITY TYPE

Personality Trait	Primary Trait			Secondary Trait			Desire for Change	
	Strength of Trait (Scale 0–10)	How Natural or Comfortable (Scale 0–10)	HowWell Works (Scale 0–10)	Strength of Trait (Scale 0–10)	How Natural or Comfortable (Scale 0–10)	HowWell Works (Scale 0–10)	Increase (list trait)	Decrease (list trait)
(1) Extroversion-Introversion								
(2) Sensing-Intuition								
(3) Thinking-Feeling								
(4) Judging-Perceiving								

Part 1. Extroversion versus Introversion

Now, on the mental screen in front of you, notice the two words—Extroversion and Introversion. They represent the way you focus your attention. You see the words flashing on the screen, and you see a picture below each word. In the picture below "Extroversion," you see images of people socializing and talking. In the picture below "Introversion," you see images suggesting ideas, thought, and reflection. Look at these pictures for a few moments and then notice the words above each picture again. As you watch, you notice that one word gradually begins flashing brighter and brighter.

Focus on that word and select it. As you do, the picture below it fades, and now as you gaze at that blank screen, ask to see some scenes from your own life in which you have expressed that quality of Extroversion or Introversion. See them flash by like a slide show of images. As they do, notice how you feel about these images. Do you feel very comfortable and natural? Or do you feel as if you are playing a role? Notice how easily the images come to you. Is this the way you usually are? . . . Now see the slide show coming to the end and let the screen go blank.

Then look at the word for the opposite quality. If you looked at Extroversion before, look at Introversion now. Or if you looked at Introversion before, look at Extroversion now. Now focus on this word, and, as you do, ask to see some scenes from your life in which you have expressed this quality of Extroversion or Introversion. Again, see these scenes flash by like a slide show. As they do, notice how you feel. Do you feel very comfortable and natural? Or do you feel as if you are playing a role? Notice how easily the images come to you. Is this the way you usually are? . . . Now see the slide show coming to the end and let the screen go blank.

Now think about the two series of images. Which of the two feels more comfortable or natural? Which had the most images? Which images came more easily to you? This represents your more usual mode of focusing your attention—outward or inward. The first word you selected was probably your more usual approach, but it might be the way you would like to be. Maybe the other approach was more comfortable, natural, and typical of you. Notice if this is so.

Now, drawing on the experience you have just had, ask yourself the following questions. Let the first thought that comes to you be your answer; write it down.

➤ What is your more usual way of focusing your attention: Extroversion or Introversion?

On a scale of 0–10:

➤ How strongly do you feel you express this?

➤ How comfortably or naturally do you feel you express this?

➤ How well do you feel this orientation works for you?

➤ Now, taking the other way of focusing your attention, how strongly do you feel you express this?

➤ How comfortably or naturally do you feel you express this?

➤ How well do you feel this orientation works for you?

Finally, reflect on these questions:

➤ How do you feel about the balance between your qualities of Extroversion and Introversion?

➤ Is there anything you want to change? Do you want to become less Extroverted or less Introverted? More Extroverted or more Introverted? Do you want to develop more or fewer of these qualities in certain situations? Or do you like the way you are now?

As you reflect on these questions, notice what answers come to you.

Then, when you feel ready, let go of these reflections and return to the room.

Part 2. Sensing versus Intuition

Now, on the mental screen in front of you, notice the two words—Sensing and Intuition. They represent the way you acquire information. You see them flashing on the screen, and you see a picture below each word. In the picture below "Sensing," you see images of objects and things. In the picture below "Intuition," you see more abstract images or impressions, representing concepts or ideas. Look at these pictures for a few moments and then notice the words above each picture again. As you watch, you notice that one word gradually begins flashing brighter and brighter.

Focus on that word and select it. As you do, the picture below it fades, and now as you gaze at that blank screen, ask to see some scenes from your own life in which you gained knowledge through Sensing or Intuition. See them flash by like a slide show of images. As they do, notice how you feel about these images. Do you feel very comfortable and natural? Is it difficult for you to gain information this way? Notice how easily the images come to you. Is this the way you usually obtain information? . . . Now see the slide show coming to the end and let the screen go blank.

Then look at the word for the opposite quality. If you looked at Sensing before, look at Intuition now. If you looked at Intuition before, look at Sensing now. Focus on this word, and, as you do, ask to see some scenes from your life in which you gained knowledge through your Sensing or Intuition. Again, see these scenes flash by like a slide show. As they do, notice how you feel. Do you feel very comfortable and natural? Or is it more difficult for you to gain information this way? Also, notice how easily the images come to you. Is this the way you usually obtain information? . . . Now see the slide show coming to the end and let the screen go blank.

Now think about the two series of images. Which of the two feels more comfortable or natural? Which had the most images? In which did the images come more easily? This represents your more usual mode of gaining information. Probably the first word you selected was your more usual approach, but it might be the way you would like to be. Maybe the other approach was more comfortable, natural, and typical of you. Notice which is more true for you.

Now, drawing on the experience you have just had, ask yourself the following questions. Let the first thought that comes to you be your answer; write it down.

➤ What is your more usual way of gaining information: Sensing or Intuition?

On a scale of 0-10:

➤ How strongly do you feel you express this?

➤ How comfortably or naturally do you feel you express this?

➤ How well do you feel this orientation works for you?

➤ Now, taking the other way of gaining information, how strongly do you feel you express this?

➤ How comfortably or naturally do you feel you express this?

➤ How well do you feel this orientation works for you?

Finally, reflect on these questions:

➤ How do you feel about the balance between your qualities of Sensing and Intuition?

➤ Is there anything you want to change? Do you want to become less Sensing or less Intuitive? More Sensing or more Intuitive? Do you want to develop more or fewer of these qualities in certain situations? Or do you like the way you are now?

As you reflect on these questions, notice what answers come to you.

Then, when you feel ready, let go of these reflections and return to the room.

Part 3. Thinking versus Feeling

On the mental screen in front of you, notice the two words—Thinking and Feeling. They represent the way you make decisions. You see them flashing on the screen, and you see a picture below each word. In the picture below "Thinking," you see the image of a scientist, professor, or a manager reviewing information. In the picture below "Feeling," you see yourself in a warm, comfortable setting, in which you can easily make decisions based on how you feel about the situation. Look at these pictures for a few moments and then notice the words above each picture again. As you watch, you notice that one word gradually begins flashing brighter and brighter.

Focus on that word and select it. As you do, the picture below it fades, and now as you gaze at that blank screen, ask to see some scenes from your own life when you made a decision using that style of Thinking or Feeling. See these scenes flash by you like a slide show of images. As they do, notice how you feel about these images. Do you feel very comfortable and natural? Do you like making decisions this way? Do you feel they are good decisions? Notice how easily the images come to you. Is this the way you make decisions? . . . Now see the slide show coming to the end and let the screen go blank.

Then look at the word for the opposite quality. If you looked at Thinking before, look at Feeling now. If you looked at Feeling before, look at Thinking now. Now focus on this word, and, as you do, ask to see some scenes from your life in which you made a decision using that style of Thinking or Feeling. Again, see these scenes flash by you like a slide show. As they do, notice how you feel. Does this feel very comfortable and natural? Do you like making decisions this way? Do you feel they are good decisions? Notice how easily the images come. Is this the way you usually obtain information? . . . Now see the slide show coming to the end and let the screen go blank.

Now think about the two series of images you have seen. Notice which of the two feels more comfortable or natural to you. Which had the most images? In which did the images came more easily? This represents your more usual mode of making decisions. Probably the first word you selected was your more usual approach, but it might be the way you would like to be; maybe the other approach was more comfortable, natural, and typical of you. Notice which is more true for you.

Now, drawing on the experience you have just had, ask yourself the following questions. Let the first thought that comes to you be your answer; write it down.

➤ What is your more usual way of making decisions: Thinking or Feeling?

On a scale of 0-10:

➤ How strongly do you feel you express this?

➤ How comfortably or naturally do you feel you express this?

➤ How well do you feel this orientation works for you?

➤ Now, taking the other way of making decisions, how strongly do you feel you express this?

➤ How comfortably or naturally do you feel you express this?

➤ How well do you feel this orientation works for you?

Finally, reflect on these questions:

➤ How do you feel about the balance between your qualities of Thinking and Feeling?

➤ Is there anything you want to change? Do you want to become less Thinking or less Feeling? More Thinking or more Feeling? Do you want to develop more or fewer of these qualities in certain situations? Or do you like the way you are now?

As you reflect on these questions, notice what answers come to you.

Then, when you feel ready, let go of these reflections and return to the room.

Part 4. Judging versus Perceiving

On the mental screen in front of you, notice the two words—Judging and Perceiving. They represent the way you orient yourself toward the outside world. You see them flashing on the screen, and you see a picture below each word. In the picture below "Judging," you see the image of a very orderly room or environment where everything is very neat and organized. In the picture below "Perceiving," you see the image of a room or setting where things are less clear, less organized, shifting and changing. Look at these pictures for a few moments, and then notice the words above each picture again. As you watch, you notice that one word gradually begins flashing brighter and brighter.

Focus on that word and select it. As you do, the picture below it fades, and now as you gaze at that blank screen, ask to see some scenes from your own life in which you reacted to a situation by using that orientation of Judging or Perceiving. See these scenes flash by you like a slide show of images. As they do, notice how you feel about these images. Do you feel very comfortable and natural? Or do these images seem unusual or foreign to you? Also, notice how easily the images come to you. Is this the way you usually relate to the world around you? . . . Now see the slide show coming to the end and let the screen go blank.

Then look at the word for the opposite quality. If you looked at Judging before, look at Perceiving now. If you looked at Perceiving before, look at Judging now. Now focus on this word, and, as you do, ask to see some scenes from your life in which you responded to a situation by using that response of Judging or Perceiving. Again, see these scenes flash by you like a slide show. As they do, notice how you feel about these images. Do you feel very comfortable and natural? Or do these images seem strange or distant to you? How do you like responding this way? How do you like the results? Also, notice how easily the images come to you. Is this the way you usually obtain information? . . . Now see the slide show coming to the end and let the screen go blank.

Now think about the two series of images you have just seen. Notice which of the two feels more comfortable or natural. Which had the most images? In which did the images come more easily? This represents your more usual way of relating and responding to the world around you. Probably the first word you selected was your more usual approach, but it might be the way you would like to be. Maybe the other approach was more comfortable, natural, and typical of you. Notice which is true for you.

And now, drawing on the experience you have just had, ask yourself the following questions. Let the first thought that comes to you be your answer; write it down.

➤ What is your more usual way of relating to the world around you: Judging or Perceiving?

On a scale of 0–10:

➤ How strongly do you feel you express this?

➤ How comfortably or naturally do you feel you express this?

➤ How well do you feel this orientation works for you?

➤ Now, taking the other way of relating to the world, how strongly do you feel you express this?

➤ How comfortably or naturally do you feel you express this?

➤ How well do you feel this orientation works for you?

Finally, reflect on these questions:

➤ How do you feel about the balance between your qualities of Judging and Perceiving?

➤ Is there anything you want to change? Do you want to become less Judging or less Perceiving? More Judging or more Perceiving? Do you want to develop more or fewer of these qualities in certain situations? Or do you like the way you are now?

As you reflect on these questions, notice what answers come to you.

Then, when you feel ready, let go of these reflections and return to the room.

■Identifying Specific Traits and Targeting Change

So far we've talked about general personality traits. You may want to change particular characteristics. If, for example, you have trouble being authoritative—you feel uncomfortable being in charge because you aren't sure people will follow your directions—you can visualize yourself being more powerful and authoritative, showing more leadership in your position. Or say you have difficulty in controlling your temper with a particular person or in a particular situation, you can imagine your way to controlling your anger and becoming a team player.

The following exercise will help you identify those characteristics you want to eliminate and those you want to adopt.

Exercise 20

IDENTIFYING THE PERSONALITY TRAITS YOU WANT TO CHANGE

(Time: 10–15 minutes)

Copy the chart on page 121. Holding the paper before you, relax and close your eyes. Ask yourself, "What personality traits do I want to eliminate?" Just be receptive and see what comes to you. As ideas or images come to mind, write them down. Don't try to judge whether you can get rid of that trait. Keep going until you have listed at least five traits or have started to slow down.

Then ask: "What difficult situations have I encountered in the past few weeks?" Again, be receptive; see what comes. As each scene appears, notice how you are acting and whether anything you are doing has been making this situation difficult for you. If so, this is probably a personality trait you will want to change. Write this personality trait in the first column. Keep going until you start to slow down.

Next, ask yourself the question: "What traits do I want to acquire?" In some cases, these traits may be the reverse of those you want to eliminate; in other cases, they may be entirely different ones. Whatever comes to you is fine. Just list them in the second column. Don't critique or evaluate the trait. And don't try to judge whether or not you can realistically acquire that trait. Again, keep going until you have listed at least five traits or have started to slow down.

Finally, ask: "What new situations would I like to be in, where I am different from what I am now?" Again be receptive and see what comes. As each scene appears, notice what personality traits you have that are making the situation feel very comfortable and natural. These may be personality qualities you want to acquire but don't have now. Write down in the third column any of these qualities that come up for you Keep going until you start to slow down.

When you feel finished, you are ready to set priorities. Which traits do you want to eliminate or develop first? Look down the list of traits you want to eliminate; for each one, come up with the complementary or opposite trait you would like to acquire and list it in the second column (if you haven't already listed that trait in the third column). Then, after you have listed this complementary trait or found it in the third column, cross out the trait you want to eliminate from the first column.

Now, look down the list of all the traits in columns two and three and set priorities. To do so, rate each trait from 0 (low priority) to 3 (high priority). Finally, look at the traits you have marked with the highest priority category. Should you have more than one or two traits in this category, go through this list and rank them again, until you have selected one or two traits that are the most important to you. If there are two, note which is more important to you.

You have now established your priorities, so you can work first on developing the quality that is most important to you. Should you wish, you can work on acquiring two qualities, but it's best not to work on more than two at a time. Once you feel certain you have made these a part of your personality, you can go on to the next traits on your list in order of priority. When you feel you've completed these and incorporated them into your personality, you may want to make a new list.

Changing Your Personality Traits

After you have identified the general and specific personality traits you want to change, you can work on changing either your overall orientation, specific traits, or both, but don't try to change more than two or three things about yourself at a time. Remember, your global personality traits represent your more general approach to relating to others and the world and reflect how you perceive information or make decisions. The particular personality traits reflect specific behavioral patterns and responses, which may be part of a larger pattern.

IDENTIFYING THE PERSONALITY TRAITS
I WANT TO CHANGE

Traits I Want to Eliminate	Complementary Traits I Want to Acquire	Other Traits I Want to Acquire	Priority Rating (Scale 0–3)

■Mental Scripting: How to See Yourself as You Want to Be

Now that you have identified the personality traits you want to eliminate or acquire, you have a good baseline for thinking about what you want to change and who you want to become. You know the qualities you want to develop or eliminate and the specific traits you want to acquire. Now you can work on eliminating or acquiring these traits.

A good way to do this is through mental scripting to create new patterns and approaches in your mind that you can then play out in "real" life.

How Mental Scripting Works

Mental scripting to develop or eliminate personality traits is much like the mental rehearsal technique used to practice a particular skill or ability. In this case, however, you create a more detailed scenario in which you mentally play out a desired role again and again until you create a habit or pattern of action. As you repeatedly experience the action mentally, you reinforce the pattern in your mind. This, in turn, makes you feel more and more certain you can play the role, and that confidence carries over into playing the scene in everyday life. You are a movie director creating a scene for your own movie; you create the setting in which you play out your imagined script and possess the personality traits you desire.

For example, if you want to be more assertive and authoritative at work in order to advance your career, picture yourself as more assertive and authoritative in your present position and see others respond to you in a more cooperative, agreeable way, acknowledging your desired leadership ability. Specifically, you might see yourself giving instructions clearly and firmly, imagine others listening to you more seriously, and experience others coming to you for advice, having recognized your authority and expertise. You might also project yourself into the future and see yourself expressing the desired leadership qualities in the position you want. You might see yourself in your new office, feeling very comfortable, and imagine yourself doing the tasks you want to do, such as giving instructions to your staff, attending a board meeting, and flying to see an important client. In response, people defer to you and respect you in your new role.

The following exercise will help you create a mental script.

Exercise 21

CREATING A MENTAL SCRIPT: BE WHO YOU WANT TO BE

(Time: 5–10 minutes)

Decide which trait you want to work on changing or acquiring. As usual, get relaxed and close your eyes. Take a minute or two to focus on your breathing to get very calm and relaxed.

Then, with that trait you want to change or acquire in mind, imagine a setting in which you want to express that trait—at work, at home, with friends, anywhere. Tell yourself that you now have the trait you desire and see yourself expressing that trait in that setting in the present. You have been in the situation before, but now you are acting in this new way. See yourself vividly doing so. Notice the environment around you. Notice the colors, the people around you, the smells, the objects. Experience yourself interacting, talking with others. As you do, remind yourself that you have this quality you want to have, and you feel very comfortable, very natural, very confident, acting this new way. Experience this for a few minutes.

Now project yourself into the future into a situation you would like to be in where you have this trait. It might be a move, a promotion, a new relationship. Whatever it is, tell yourself that you have the trait you want to have and see yourself expressing it in this future setting. You see this future scene clearly and vividly, as if it is happening now. Notice the environment around you. Notice the colors, the people around you, the smells, the objects. Experience yourself interacting, talking with others. As you do, remind yourself that you have this quality you want to have, and you feel very comfortable, very natural, very confident, acting this new way. Again, experience this for a few minutes.

When you feel ready, let go of the scene and let it fade. As it does, you feel very good, very confident, ready to put this new trait into practice.

Then, holding in your mind that feeling and enthusiasm to go out and do it, return to the room. Count backwards from 5 to 1, and as you do, you will come back. Five, four, becoming more and more alert. Three, two, almost back. And one. You are back in the room.

Practicing Your Mental Script

Once you have created a mental script you like, practice applying it in the real world. Practice it a few minutes a day, until you really feel that new trait becomes a part of you.

For example, if you have imagined yourself being more authoritative in the work place, go to work with this idea firmly in mind. You may want to replay a scene from your script so you can see yourself. Then, should an appropriate situation arise, assert yourself; be firm. As you do, remember the feeling of confidence you felt as you asserted yourself in your mental script.

Turning Your Mental Script into Everyday Reality

In the beginning, you may have to pay extra attention to your mental script and keep reminding yourself that you are trying to change by substituting a new way of feeling and acting for an old one. You may need to replay parts of your script from time to time and pay careful attention to what you say and do in order to break old patterns and replace them with your new ones. Eventually, as you keep inserting your new scripting into the way you act, it will become a habit, and after awhile, you won't need to use the script anymore. The new trait and your behavior reflecting this trait will have become a part of you.

CHAPTER 9

NATURAL MIND BOOSTERS
Become Smarter, Think Better

Smart drinks and nutrients have become all the rage, not only to provide more energy (see Chapter 4), but because people want to know more and think better in today's competitive, information-exploding world. Smart drinks and nutrients help them boost their memory, learn faster, and be more attentive and alert.

Similarly, your inner creative powers can sharpen your thinking and mental agility. They can make you more focused, alert, and aware, so your ability to learn and remember improves. They can also help you react more quickly and process more information. This, in turn, increases your ability to think and helps you go after and get what you want.

▮Natural Mind Boosters to Improve Your Memory and Ability to Learn

There are many ways you can benefit from increasing your ability to learn, remember, and process information. These techniques will help you to

➤ remember tasks so you don't forget to do anything that's really important;

➤ remember the small, but important, details and supplement any notes or mental comments you made or had at the time;

➤ recall the names of people met at social and business functions;

➤ improve your presentations at speeches, workshops, or seminars, with a better recall of jokes and stories as well as facts and figures and anything else you need;

➤ better your test scores;

➤ excel at job interviews, since you'll better remember what to say and how to say it.

Undoubtedly, you can think of dozens of other benefits.

Why do you want to know or remember more? Make a list of your own reasons. It will help motivate you to improve your own abilities. Use the chart on page 127 and write down all the reasons you have for wanting to know and remember more. Then, as you work with the exercises described in this section, you can direct your improved abilities to these purposes.

Before you start writing, get in a relaxed and receptive frame of mind. Then, ask yourself these questions: "Why do I want to know and remember more?" "How can I apply knowing and remembering more in my own life?" Write down the reasons as quickly as you can. Then rate them from 0 (low) to 5 (high) to indicate your priorities.

∎Improve Your Concentration with Active-Focusing Techniques

Alison had trouble in college: she found it hard to pay attention to lectures. As she listened, she grew restless; her mind would drift, until suddenly, she would realize she had drifted off and would pull herself back. By then, though, she had missed several minutes of the lecture and found it hard to get back into

WHY I WANT TO KNOW AND REMEMBER MORE

Reason	Rating (Scale 0–5)

it. In a few minutes, she would drift off again. She had done the same thing as a child when her parents took her to church and she found it difficult to pay attention to the sermon. In church, she didn't get caught; no one tested her on the information she had missed; but now in college, her drifting off had become a serious matter.

Finally, Alison overcame the problem by using an active-focusing technique that kept her attention on the speaker and forced her to hear and process what was being said.

Three Concentration-Boosting Techniques

Alison's problem is not unique. If you have this problem, try one of these active-focusing techniques to help maintain your concentration and focus.

1. *Take notes.* If you have a sheet of paper or notebook handy, write down the key points the person is making. Even if you don't read your notes later, the act of writing them will focus your attention and help you absorb more information. Some people find that detailed notes help them better understand and think about what they hear. Others find a lot of writing interferes with their concentration and just jot down main phrases and concepts. Try both methods to determine which works best for you.

2. *React to and comment mentally on what you hear.* We can think about what we hear without interfering with concentration because we think several times faster than people speak. That allows us to think thoughts in the empty spaces between. As we do, our minds connect what we think with what we hear, so that it feels as if we are doing both at the same time. By actively thinking while you listen, you force yourself to pay more attention since you are processing and responding to information, not just taking it in.

3. *Use a physical trigger or focus your attention.* A gesture or physical signal can remind you to pay attention to what you are hearing. A soft click of your fingers, moving a toe or another part

of your body can act as a reminder to stay focused. With some practice, this signal can become an automatic attention focuser.

∎Improve Your Memory with the Associated-Image Technique

Phil, a manager of a small company, had trouble remembering the names of people he met at the many business meetings and social functions he attended. He usually returned home from one of these events with plenty of business cards, but within a day or two, he couldn't remember who was who. They were just names; he couldn't remember what they had talked about. Even when he took quick notes, it didn't help much. The notes might remind him to send someone some information, but the rest of the exchange was gone.

Finally, Phil started using an associated image or word to help him remember. These words or images were based on a feature that stood out or on something the person said—an unusual name, a striking physical characteristic, a unique hobby. Phil would replay the image in his mind as he heard the person's name and as they spoke. Later, when he went through the business cards he had collected, the person's name triggered the image and the main points of the conversation. He then had a clear picture of the person and what he should do. If he didn't followup immediately, he made a detailed note (including the word or image) on the person's card.

How to Use the Associated-Image Technique

To use this technique to help you remember something, do the following:

1. Whenever you meet someone, think of an image or word you associate with that person. Base it on something unique about that person (such as his or her name, appearance, or an interest).

2. Repeat that word or see that image several times as you talk to the person.

3. If you get the person's business card, note the word or image on the card.

∎The Power of Mental Imagery to Affect Brain Functioning

Like smart drugs and nutrients, mental imagery works to improve brain function by changing the chemical balance in the brain. This, in turn, increases the flow of thoughts through the nerve cells. Thoughts are transmitted through the brain as electrical impulses, and these impulses affect the chemistry of the brain. (Research on pain, for example, has shown that positive thinking can increase the amount of endorphins, which act to increase pleasure and reduce pain.) By the same token, certain mental imagery can stimulate nerve-cell firing and the action of the neurotransmitters, which promotes the flow of information through the brain. While mental imagery can be used in conjunction with smart drugs and nutrients to help supplement their effect, it can also be used by itself to stimulate the brain functioning that produces improved learning, memory, and thinking.

To understand the ways in which mental imagery increases brain functioning, let's review how the brain processes information.

How Memories Are Created

According to researchers, we have three types of memory:

1. *Short-term memory*—when you remember something for a matter of seconds, such as the name of a person you just met a party or someone's telephone number.

2. *Long-term memory*—the deeper impression that occurs when we experience or think about something often enough or deeply enough that it becomes etched in our minds, so we can recall it at will.

3. *Working memory*—the ability to store important information for a short period of time, recall it, and forget it, if necessary.[1]

---

[1] Ross Pelton, *Mind Food & Smart Pills*, New York: Doubleday, 1989, pp. 39–42.

Although scientists are still debating exactly how memories are created and recorded in the brain, they generally believe the input of a memory triggers some sort of change in the structure of the neuron or group of neurons.[2] Presumably, a short-term memory might produce a temporary or insignificant change, while a long-term memory might lead to a permanent and/or deeper change in this structure, resulting in a corresponding change in the way these structures process information.

Researchers also believe that the neurotransmitter chemicals in the brain play a key role in creating these different types of memories and that the electrical signals in the brain interact with these neurotransmitters: A sufficient supply of these transmitters helps the neurons function effectively; an insufficient supply can interfere with their functioning. Some researchers believe that an optimal supply can enhance functioning.[3] Since mental imagery can help increase the supply of neurotransmitters, it can help improve memory and thinking.

Thinking and Intelligence: The Role of Mental Imagery

Researchers generally agree that there is no fixed intelligence and that one's mental functioning, including verbal ability, logical thinking skills, and response time, can be improved.[4] For example, Dr. Marian Diamond, a neuroanatomist at the University of California, found that rats raised in an enriched environment had bigger brains, could remember more, and could think better, since they could more quickly and accurately solve problems.[5] Similarly, by using mental imagery to stimulate your brain functioning, you can think and reason better.

---

[2] Pelton, p. 43.

[3] Durk Pearson and Sandy Shaw, *Life Extension*, New York: Warner Brothers, 1982, p. 126.

[4] Beverly A. Potter and J. Sebastian Orfali, *Brain Boosters: Foods and Drugs that Make You Smarter*, 1993, and Pelton, *Mind Food & Smart Pills*.

[5] Pelton, p. 63.

■Natural Memory-Building Techniques

The following techniques will help to improve your ability to remember, learn, and think in a number of ways. They will:

1. Increase your ability to pay focused attention so you initially register more information.

2. Create a strong picture or tapestry of associations, leaving a stronger memory trace.

3. Develop mental cues and other aids to retrieving memory.

Exercise 22

CREATING A MENTAL TRIGGER

(Time: 2–3 minutes)

Many people forget things because they don't pay enough attention at the outset. As a result, the picture in their minds starts out fuzzy. Though we sometimes create clear pictures from the information we unconsciously absorb (for example, you pass a person in the street and later recall details vividly, although you didn't pay much attention at the time), many times those images don't register. So if you depend on your unconscious alone to create your memories, you are taking a great chance.

When you really want to remember something, it's essential to remind yourself to pay close attention. One way to do this is to create a mental trigger to jog your memory to pay attention. This trigger can be just about anything—a physical gesture, such as touching a part of your body, a mental statement you make to yourself, and the like. What should you use? If you already have a signal you like, use that. If not, try the following exercise to create your own trigger (it will also help reinforce your current signal).

As usual, get comfortable, close your eyes and relax. Concentrate on your breathing for a minute or two to feel really relaxed.

Then, ask yourself: "What mental trigger would I like to use to remind myself to pay attention?" What comes into your mind? It may be a gesture, a physical movement, a mental image, or a word or phrase you say to yourself. Choose that as your trigger.

To give power to this trigger, make the gesture or movement or let this image or word appear in your mind. As you make this gesture or observe the image or word, say to yourself with increasing intensity: "I will pay attention now . . . I will pay attention now . . . I will pay attention now . . . I will remember this (experience/statement/person/you fill in what you want to remember)." Repeat this statement to yourself several times.

Later in the day or the next day, try using this trigger in some everyday situations. When you see something you would like to remember (such as someone on the street, a car on the road, and so forth), use your trigger to remind you to pay attention to it. Then, later, when whatever you have seen is gone, replay it mentally in as much detail as possible to illustrate how much you can remember when you really pay attention.

Keep repeating both parts of this exercise (the visualization and the real-life practice) over the next week, so you really lock in your desire to pay attention with the trigger you have chosen. Once this connection is solidified and you continue to use the trigger from time to time, you won't need to practice the exercise. The trigger will bring up the association (to pay attention) and that's what you will do. Then, anytime you want to be especially focused or remember things, use your mental trigger. It will help you stay more focused and alert.

Exercise 23

CREATING IMAGES WITH IMPACT—SEE LIKE A CAMERA, LISTEN LIKE A TAPE RECORDER

(Time: 3–5 minutes each part)

In addition to paying attention, remembering well depends on making a clear and sharp mental picture of what you want to remember. Otherwise, it's easy to incorrectly fill in the details later, so that we think we really have remembered something, when, in fact, we are just imagining that memory.

One way to get a very clear impression of something is to think of yourself as a camera or tape recorder, making a very clear picture or recording of what you are experiencing. Then, when it comes time to remember, imagine yourself seeing that picture or film or listening to that tape.

The following exercises are designed to help you practice and apply this ability. Initially, use the exercises to create a baseline for what you usually remember. As you practice, you'll find you can picture or record more and more details and recall them. The basic approach of these exercises is to observe or listen to something for a short time, stop observing or listening, and recall what you can. Then, when you look or listen again, notice how much you remembered, how much you forgot, and how much you created that wasn't there. With practice, you'll increase how much you remember, reduce how much you forgot, and be less likely to create or embroider memories that aren't. As you improve with practice, and these approaches to remembering become part of you, you'll find this skill will carry over into other situations, and you'll automatically start making more accurate memory pictures or recordings.[6] Use the chart on page 137 to help chart your accuracy and progress over time.

Part 1. Looking More Accurately

(Time: 3–5 minutes)

Look at a scene in front of you that has many different things in it. These can be different objects, people who are mostly stationary (that is, sitting down, not a bustling crowd), scenery, and so forth. Or look at a picture of such a scene. Then stare at this scene for about a minute and, as you do, imagine you are taking a picture of it. Notice as many things about the scene as you can. Pay attention to forms, colors, the number of objects or people there, the relationship between things, and so on.

Then look away from the scene and try to re-create it as accurately as possible in your mind's eye. Again, notice the forms, colors, number of objects or people, the relationship between things.

Next, to check your accuracy, without looking back, write down what you saw in as much detail as possible.

Finally, how accurate and complete was your memory? Rate your observations. To score your level of accuracy, look at the actual scene. Give each accurate observation a score of +2. Give each inaccurate

---

[6] These are adapted from *Mind Power*, pp. 88–90.

observation a–1. Give each invented observation a–2. Tally your scores and note the result. To score your level of accuracy, look around, and estimate the total number of observations you think were possible in the scene and divide by the number of observations you made. (A mental or written list will help you keep track.) As you continue to practice with this exercise, you'll find your score for both accuracy and completeness should go up.

Part 2. Listening More Accurately

(Time: 3–5 minutes)

As you listen to a conversation, tape a few minutes of it on a tape recorder. Choose a real conversation or a television or radio program. As you tape the conversation, concentrate on listening as intently and carefully as possible. Imagine you are a tape recorder that is recording every bit of conversation clearly and accurately.

Then try to recall the conversation in as much detail as possible. You may want to imagine yourself as a tape recorder playing the tape back.

Next, to check your accuracy, write down what you heard in as much detail as possible.

Finally, rate your accuracy and completeness by rating your recall. To score your level of accuracy, designate each accurate recollection with a+2. Score each inaccurate recollection with a–1. Score each invented recollection with a–2. Then tally your score and note the result. To score your level of accuracy, listen to the actual tape of that conversation or program, and, as you listen, estimate the total number of recollections you might have made listening to that tape and divide by the number of recollections you actually made. As you continue to practice with this exercise, you'll find your score for both accuracy and completeness should go up.

Besides practicing and testing your ability to see and listen more closely under experimental conditions, you can use this approach in everyday situations—particularly when you are in a situation where it is very important to get and recall complete information.

You'll also find impromptu situations where you can sharpen your skills by informally practicing and getting a rough idea of how accurate and complete your memory is. If you are waiting in line, sitting at a train station or airport, waiting to go into a meeting or interview, try looking around or listening to what's going on. Imagine that you are a camera or tape recorder, see how much detail you can record; then turn away from the scene or stop listening, and reflect on what you experienced; try to recall as much as you can. Afterward, look back and think about how accurate you were. It's good practice.

■Memory Retrieval Techniques: Mental Cues and Other Aids

Once you have done all you can to pay attention to and firmly imprint an impression—whether visual, auditory, or some other sense—the final step is doing all you can to recall it. Retrieval is easiest when you have made a clear initial impression of something, since the memory trace is brighter, louder, or otherwise more intense, so you can see, hear, or experience it better. But even if you have only imprinted something slightly or the trace has faded, these retrieval techniques will help you tap your unconscious, so you can dig back, even into the more flimsy impressions, to retrieve it.

Every impression, every sensation, no matter how minor, makes some kind of imprint on the neurons in your brain. Researchers have found that tapping certain parts of the brain, using special probes, triggers certain memories. Though the process isn't fully understood, it's believed that every image we see, every sound or conversation we hear, every experience we have, gets registered someplace in the brain. Although most of these impressions fade from consciousness and many are just lightly recorded, they are there, somewhere. That's why certain processes, like hypnosis and deep concentration, as well as physical stimuli, can pull these back. The less clear, more faded impressions will be harder to tap, since they are so much fainter. But they are still there.

HOW ACCURATE AND COMPLETE IS MY MEMORY?

Things I Observed or Heard	Accurate (+2)	Inaccurate (-1)	Invented (-2)

Totals:

Completeness Score:____
Estimated Possibilities:____
Items Recalled:____

Accuracy Score (Accurate-
Inaccurate and
Invented Scores):____

One good way to trigger a memory is to try to go back to or re-create the time when the impression was first created. This intense focus helps to pull up the memory, something like making the memory live again. Instead of an abstract, detached perception of what is there, you are reliving what's there; you are making the memory come alive; you are making it more intensely, vividly real.

For example, to recall a name, imagine the person before you, and perhaps recall your first meeting. To recall a phone number, visualize a time when you looked up the number in a book, wrote down the number on a piece of paper, or dialed it. To recall where you put some object, imagine yourself in the situation where you last had the object and notice what you did with it when you put it down. To recall a route, imagine yourself in the car or on foot traveling along it from where you started. To recall some information from a book or movie, visualize yourself reading the book or watching the film. To recall what happened at an event, imagine yourself there and play out the scene in your mind.

In short, the key to recalling things is to turn an abstract thought into a vivid picture, drawing on as many of your senses as possible, so you in effect re-create the original experience. By seeing and experiencing that incident, you can recall much more than you otherwise could.

∎Three Thinking and Learning Techniques

You can improve your ability to think and learn by:

1. Increasing your ability to pay attention, concentrate, and make the information you receive more vivid, which helps you absorb and process more information in the first place;

2. Increasing your ability to make connections between things, so you can better relate different pieces of information;

3. Increasing your ability to maintain your interest, so you can take in more information.

Exercise 24

ACTIVELY LISTENING AND SEEING

(Time: 30 seconds—1 minute for reminder; then however long you practice doing this during the event)

In addition to reminding yourself to pay attention, say by using a mental trigger, you need to be able to stay attentive and focused. One way to do this is to not only passively receive the information you are taking in—visual, auditory, or otherwise—but to *actively respond* to this information as you receive it. You can do this, particularly when you listen to information, because there is a lag between the time needed to take in information and the time needed to register it in your mind.

For example, when you listen to a lecture or a conversation, the person talks at about one third or one quarter the rate at which you can think. You can use the additional time to actively reflect on what the person is saying—for example, with a mental commentary. The time lag between speaking and thinking also allows you to take detailed notes while still listening to the speaker; you are in effect writing between the spaces. Both your own mental commentary and the process of note taking help focus your attention. In addition, by encoding the information in another sensory channel, you create another track for imprinting the information in your mind, allowing you to learn and remember more. Thus, if you take notes at a lecture, even if you never look at them again, you get more information and remember it better, because you not only hear information and pay more attention to it, but you make it visual, too, by writing it down, and you create another memory channel.

It is possible to actively respond and encode the information into another channel simultaneously. For example, as you make notes, you can also create a mental commentary about what the person is saying. This dual process increases your ability to learn by making the information that much more vivid. By increasing the impressions made in your mind, you learn and remember more.

These techniques can also be used to remember information gained through observation. As you look at something, reflect on what you are seeing. Talk to yourself about what you are seeing and what you think and feel about it. Perhaps compare what you are seeing now to something else you have seen that looks the same or looks different.

Try putting this way of responding to information into practice. Before you go to a lecture or speak with someone, remind yourself that you will actively react in your mind to what is said, and, if you expect to take notes, remind yourself that you will make them as detailed as possible. You will also actively react in your mind to what the person is saying and what you are writing. If you go to see something (for example, an art gallery, a sightseeing trip), remind yourself that you will actively think about what you are seeing and compare and contrast it with other things. In short, before you do something where you want to be better able to focus, concentrate, and learn more, remind yourself to approach the experience in receiving and perceiving mode, so that you actively react to what you are seeing. You may also want to incorporate this information in another sensory channel as well.

Exercise 25 _____

MAKING CONNECTIONS

(Time: 3–5 minutes for mind mapping; time varies for how you apply the technique in different situations)

By increasing your ability to make connections between things and relate different pieces of information, you are, in effect, facilitating the flow of information in your brain. These increased connections can be very useful on a day-to-day basis, since they can suggest new ideas, new uses for things, intuitive leaps about how to improve things, and so forth.

How do you increase your ability to make connections? One way is by practicing more associative thinking. You think of one thing and actively try to imagine all the things it suggests. Then you can spin off from one or more of these things to come up with still more things. It's a form of brainstorming except that the emphasis is on making associations with previous ideas rather than just coming up with any idea. The ideas grow out of an initial idea like the branches of a tree, which may have still more branches, and so on. This approach is sometimes referred to as "mind mapping."

1. Copy the chart on page 142 and write down the first word or topic that comes to mind. Put this word or phrase in the center. Next, what do you associate with that word? Write down the first things that occur to you in the first series of projections from the center.

Now, taking each of these words or phrases in turn, what are the first things that come to mind? Write these down. Keep going as long as you like (and add your own branches if necessary).

2. For additional practice, as you do things in daily life and have some time (for example, while waiting for a bus or standing in line), try coming up with associations for the things or people you see around you. Where does the chain of associations take you? If certain associations stand out, use these to continue the chain.

Later, you can apply this technique to specific situations where associative thinking can be especially helpful, such as coming up with new ideas for projects, new ways to use something you already have, and so forth.

Exercise 26

MAINTAINING YOUR INTEREST

(Time: 30 seconds–2 minutes)

Should you find your interest flagging as you try to pay attention, concentrate, or make connections, try taking a quick mental break to boost your energy and keep you focused. Like the runner who stops for a moment on the track to take a quick swig of an energy drink to get that energy boost, you may need a quick infusion of mental energy to stay involved. It's important to remember that this is just a quick break—a few seconds; at most, a minute or two. Afterwards, you have to get back on the track and start concentrating again—ideally, with even more enthusiasm and focus than before your brief break.

Here are a few suggestions for quick mental energy breaks. (You'll think of many others.)

1. Say *"Time Out."* Then glance around for a few seconds, taking mental pictures. Imagine yourself getting a charge of energy from each picture. When you refocus on your task, imagine that this energy charge is spreading through you, giving you more and more energy to continue what you are doing.

2. As you look at the person who is talking, think of something funny—a statement, image, or joke that might fit that person. Smile or laugh silently to yourself. Then, after a few seconds of

MAKING CONNECTIONS

_____

_____

_____

_____

_____

_____   _____   _____

_____   _____   _____

_____   _____   _____   _____

_____   _____   _____

_____   _____   _____

_____

_____

_____

_____

_____

comic relief, feel energized and ready to continue listening in a more serious vein.

3. Try this quick-energy recharging exercise: Think of an image of power and energy (a professional athlete, picture of a rocket, flashing neon sign saying "Energy") and, as you do, tell yourself an energy-increasing affirmation, such as "I am feeling energized . . . I am feeling energized . . . I feel more power and energy than ever . . . I feel more power and energy than ever." Then, return to your task feeling recharged and ready to go.

CHAPTER 10

TUNE INTO PEOPLE
The Power of Mind Reading

Our intuition often gives us insights into people that, if we are aware of them, can guide our reactions to them. How many times would you really have liked to know what was going on in someone's mind? Think about it: You have a job interview; you want to know the right things to say. You are making a sales presentation; you want to know what hot buttons to push. You are considering entering into a business deal with a person who sounds impressive; should you trust him?

Often, we don't recognize the cues we are picking up from others because, although the mind registers what we are sensing, we are not consciously aware of these cues. There's a real advantage to this much of the time; it protects us from sensory overload. Can you imagine having to deal with the thousands of perceptions, thoughts, feelings, and impressions that are coursing through our brain cells every moment?

But this protective process can also block us from recognizing things we want to be aware of—the little twinge of caution that tells us someone isn't telling the truth or that someone is setting a trap for us. As a result, problems can arise from missed signals.

Conversely, we can miss a great opportunity because we don't see it or act on it or we don't trust the insight we are getting. In addition, this lack of awareness can lead us to overlook the signals that let us know someone is hurt or angry at something we are saying or doing. This, in turn, can lead to conflict. And, sometimes, we may not really want to acknowledge that something is true; because the truth is so painful, we want to deny it or delay hearing it, and so block it.

■How the Desire to Believe Can Mask Warning Signals

Failing to recognize and act on these inner cues can sometimes be disastrous in a personal or business relationship. It's therefore essential to recognize a problem quickly in order to avoid or minimize the result.

Take Dave and Norma, for example. They were ready to be gullible. The signals were there, but they didn't hear them because they didn't want to notice them. As a result, they lost a lot of money in an investment scam. Here's what happened: At the invitation of friends, Dave and Norma attended a presentation of a new direct-sales program for health products. They accepted the founder's verbal assurances that, as an early investor, they would soon make thousands of dollars a month. Though they didn't fully understand the complicated business arrangements about supplies, distribution, and territory, they were impressed by the founder's smoothness, self-assurance, appearance of success, and they ignored the little warning signals that cautioned them to "check it out," such as the little twinges of confusion and uncertainty they felt as the presenter pushed on with his I-know-what-to-do-aura of authority. They so wanted to believe the man's message and to see themselves successful that they simply bought $5,000 worth of product. But after they paid their money, promised advertising and support never materialized and, after a few weeks, they found it difficult to reach the founder, who subsequently disappeared, taking most of the money with him.

Clearly, Dave and Norma should have investigated before plunging ahead. They should have asked questions. Even if they didn't understand the complicated business arrangements, they should not have been misled by the founder's outwardly professional appearance and seeming sincerity. They should have insisted on explanations they could understand, or they shouldn't have invested at all. In sum, they should have recognized that the inner-warning signal—to check it out—was urging them to see through the con man's shell and pay attention to the negative cues.

There are thousands of Daves and Normas who make mistakes about people all the time. They trust the wrong people; they don't trust the right ones. They want so much to believe the person's message that they don't pay attention to their inner messages. They are too ready to accept wrong information because it's what they want to hear, or they ignore correct information because they don't like the message. They fail to listen to the wisdom of their intuition (which may come in the form of a warning voice, a strange disturbing image, or just a gut-level feeling of distress). In fact, they may get angry and resent anyone who tries to tell them they are making a big mistake, as Dave did when I expressed some doubts about the program and the trustworthiness of the founder.

The desire to believe can be very strong. It can cloud our inner perceptions. Even someone who is normally very perceptive and intuitive about people and situations can be sucked in. Professional con artists, for example, know this and use this desire to believe to persuade people to trust them. However, if people listened to their inner voice or vision as well as to their reason, they would not fall for these scams.

How to Tune into the Danger Signals

Danger signals come in two forms:

1. an initially intense warning in the form of an inner voice, image, strange tingling sensation, or gut-level feeling that things aren't quite what they seem or the person telling you something isn't to be trusted;

2. a less intense but recurring warning in the same form.

Don't ignore this signal. Instead, ask yourself if things really are as they seem, and proceed with caution as you investigate further to see if your warning signal is correct. If you're in touch with your intuition, you will usually find it is.

■What to Do When Warning Bells Ring

Thus, as Dave and Norma's experience illustrates, the first step is to pay attention. Then, ask questions and look for underlying reasons and motivations. Therefore, you should:

1. Notice the inner-warning signals you experience, in whatever form they come to you—voices, images, or gut-level feelings.

2. Investigate the warning—ask questions, get supporting information, explanations of things you don't understand or things that seem vague or contradictory. Verify assumptions.

3. Ask yourself why you trust someone or why you believe something is true. Look for underlying reasons and motivations, which might be clouding your ability to assess the situation. Try to look behind surface appearances—seeming professionalism or slickness of the person who is trying to persuade you to do something—to get the inner truth.

4. Pay serious attention to external warnings that echo your internal warnings—or if you get external warnings first, look within to see if these warnings help to trigger your own inner warning signal.

5. If, after asking these questions, you still can't find this validating and confirming information through rational, questioning means, try tuning into your inner knowing. Put aside your desired beliefs and discover what this knowing part of you really thinks.

While much of this may seem obvious, we are often so busy that we don't have the time or energy to check every detail personally. Instead, we trust what people tell us and what friends recommend. Sometimes we so strongly want what we hear to be true that we eagerly embrace it and the people who tell it to us—and tune out those who caution us against it. That's why the inner-warning signal is so important. It's a kind of defense, advising us when to pay extra attention to something because we have unconsciously or intuitively sensed that something isn't quite right. This sense could be wrong, but it's important to pay attention to it because it is usually picking up cues we don't consciously notice, and these are the cues that signal there could be problems ahead.

How to Use Your Intuition to Get to the Truth

Outer appearances can contribute to overlooking the warnings of your inner insight. For example, people conveying the image of success and knowledge often convince others to do things on the basis of this image alone, even when there is nothing behind it. Their outer appearance is powerful enough to overcome any warning signals people may have. This is even more true when we see other people convinced by them.

It is therefore important to put aside external appearances, especially when we get repeated warning signals that things aren't quite right. We must look more closely at what's behind that outer shell.

Three Steps to Picking up Information Through Your Intuition

How do you overcome the desire to believe and the power of outside appearances? How do you check your perceptions? There are three key steps.

1. Get an accurate and clear initial impression of the person. Check this impression from time to time to see if it is still accurate. You could have made an error, or the person may have changed.

2. Recognize that the way people outwardly present themselves may differ from what they really think, feel, or believe inside. External appearance is only the outer presentation of self to

others; it is the public role we adopt. There is an inner self, too, and that inner self can be manipulative and deceptive, even though the outer self seems kind and good. When our intuition senses this discrepancy between the private and public self, it's a strong signal that we should avoid the person.

3. Be aware of what you want to believe about a person and what he or she can offer. Your desires can color what you see. Recognize that there may be disparities between what you want to believe and what is true. Look for the truth beyond your desired beliefs.

∎Step 1: Get an Accurate and Clear First Impression

When you first meet or start to work with someone, you can facilitate how you relate to each other—or you can decide whether you want to relate at all—by getting a sharp and clear overall initial impression of this person. It's like creating a quick mental resume that features the major highlights of how the person is presenting him or herself. Instead of your hearing these details from the person, however, draw on the various personal cues and clues (such as appearance, manner of speech, gestures, attitude, sense of self, and any words spoken) that a person drops to give you a capsule intuitive portrait. You can't analyze these clues quickly with your logical mind, but your intuitive mind reacts in an almost instantaneous, holistic way to create this mental portrait.

The Value of a First Impression

This portrait is based primarily on the outer person, and you should act on the assumption that the person is, in fact, who he or she appears or wants to be. Generally, the few minor discrepancies that exist between the public face we present to the world and the inner private self are not important to a good relationship. For example, the public self may reflect confidence, self-assurance, and success, while the private self is nervous, uncertain, and fearful, but, for all practical purposes, such private qualities don't interfere with the person's effective public performance.

If, as you get to know the person, you discover many minor discrepancies or any major ones between the inner and outer self, there can be problems. So in addition to using your initial intuitive impressions to guide you, it's important to be on the alert for any warning signals. Should you get warnings, check them out. As a rule, when you first meet someone, your inner antennae will pick up a true overall impression of who a person is and will disregard minor discrepancies as a kind of background noise that isn't really important. But if these discrepancies—this background noise—continues and becomes louder, pay attention. It could mean the person is presenting a false impression.

As you work with your intuition, become more aware of it, and listen to it more, you will become more sensitive to the warnings it will give you. And as you check and verify these warnings, you will gain more confidence in your intuition, which will make it more accurate.

The Sources of a First Impression

You can get a quick insight into someone in two key ways:[1]

1. your immediate auditory or visual impression (such as, appearance, gestures, attitude);

2. your first impression on physical contact (such as a handshake or a hug).

Both sources provide an overall impression, a general sense of who the person is (friendly, outgoing, shy, sensitive, creative, and the like). These insights can also help you know how to react to the person (warm and friendly; reserved; watch out—could be hard to deal with).

One way to get more detailed information is to develop your ability to get more specific initial cues. This can be done by picking up on the words or images that provide a word or visual picture

---

[1] This section is adapted from *Mind Power* and is further expanded upon.

of the person. To do this, concentrate on listening to your inner voice or on noticing any spontaneous images that appear when you meet or work with someone. These help to give you a clearer, more accurate picture of who that person is.

For example, suppose, when you are introduced to someone, you hear your inner voice say "wolf" or you see the image of a wolf briefly flash before your mind's eye. This suggests the person has the characteristics you associate with a wolf, such as being wily, aggressive, and tenacious. Or if the word or image of a "butterfly" comes to mind, this may suggest a flighty, fragile person. What's important are your own associations and meanings for that word. From this initial impression, you can take these qualities into account in dealing with the person.

Exercise 27

PICKING UP ON FIRST IMPRESSIONS

(Time: 1–2 minutes each part)

The following exercises will help you pay more detailed attention to your first impressions, as well as give you feedback on your accuracy so you can feel more confident of your abilities. This attention to your initial responses will help you become more sensitive to others and will also make you more aware of any warning signs that a person is not what he or she seems.

When you first do these exercises, jot down your impressions so you can compare your initial impressions with what you learn later about this person, from others or by getting to know him or her better. This will let you check your accuracy, which you will increase with practice. To take notes, carry a small pad or notebook with you. If you can take notes on the spot, for example at a business meeting, go ahead; otherwise, do it as soon as possible.

The three types of impressions to observe are when you first:

1. see someone from a distance;
2. meet someone in person or over the phone;
3. make an initial physical contact with someone by shaking hands.

The following exercises will help you pay more attention and get clearer, more detailed, and more accurate perceptions from these experiences.

Part 1. First Sight

This technique is ideal when you go to an event, such as a party or business meeting, and see someone you haven't yet met. It can help you to decide if this is a person you want to meet, or it can help to prepare you for when you meet by giving you some insights into the person and how to best approach or respond when you meet.

The technique: Look, in turn, at each person you want to know about and imagine that you are a camera that takes pictures that show what a person is really like. As you do, what is the first word or image that come to mind? Does any other word or image come to mind? If one comes quickly, notice if a third word or image follows quickly. Don't try to push for more words or images or go beyond two or three. Then think about what each word or image means to you. That will give you a general impression of this person. Later, after you meet the person, review your comments to see how accurate you were. It helps to write down your impressions and then the accuracy level, so you can check your accuracy over time.

Part 2. First Sound

This technique is ideal for any gathering where you meet someone in person or have a phone conversation or overhear or observe someone having a conversation with others.

The technique: As you meet, speak to, or hear the person speaking, imagine yourself as a tape recorder that has absolute fidelity and notice any words or images that pop into your mind. Then notice if any other word or image comes to mind; if one comes quickly, notice if a third word or image follows quickly. Don't try to push for more words or images or go beyond two or three. Then think about what each word or image means to you. That will give you a general impression of this person. Later, after you meet the person, review your comments to see how accurate you were. Again, it helps to write down your impressions and accuracy level, so you can check your accuracy over time.

Part 3. First Touch

This technique is ideal for when you first meet someone. Usually the first contact is a handshake.

The technique: As you shake hands, focus your awareness on that handshake and imagine that you are like a crystal that can accurately pick up the slightest vibrations or touch. As before, notice any words or images that pop into your mind. Again, notice if any other word or image comes to mind; and if one comes quickly, notice if a third word or image follows quickly; don't try to push for more words or images or go beyond two or three. Then think about what each word or image means to you. That will give you a general impression of this person. Later, after you get to know the person or get information about that person from others, review your comments to see how accurate you were. Again, it helps to write down your impressions and accuracy level, so you can check your accuracy over time.

After you work with these exercises for awhile, you will develop an automatic awareness whenever you first see, touch, or talk to someone. Over time, you won't need to use these exercises, but will find that you simply get an overall impression or message about the people you meet. This impression can range from a general feeling or sense of who the person is (trustworthy, sharp, sensitive, and the like) to more specific comments or pictures ("I think this is a sincere, loyal, honest person who has a lot of information and help to give me.").

Whatever comes, be open and receptive. As you get to know the person better, you can check out and validate these first impressions to continue refining your accuracy over time.

■Step 2: Recognize the Difference Between the Outer and Inner Self

Initial intuitive impressions provide a sense of who a person is. They are based primarily on the individual's presentation of his or her outer self and ignore minor discrepancies between the inner and outer self. There are times, however, when this difference can be significant, and it is important to recognize the differences and pay attention to early warning signals.

Understanding the Differences Between the Outer and Inner Self

The outer presentation of self is the shell we show to the world. It's the role a person chooses to play in a given situation, along with all the trappings associated with that role.

For example, a banker will act and dress a certain way, based on the social conventions that are designed to convey certain messages about the banker's role (such as being conventional, conservative, rational, organized, precise, and detail oriented). So the conservative, understated dress worn by bankers helps to reinforce that role. By contrast, a salesperson will act and dress to convey social messages associated with that role (such as being persuasive, forceful, outgoing, powerful, and friendly).

However, to truly assess a person it is necessary to cut through this outer appearance to the person underneath. In those cases where the inner person and the outer role form a good match, you'll sense alignment. The inner person will fit naturally into the outer role shell (for example, the naturally outgoing person who goes into sales; the more quiet, reserved person who goes into banking).

In other cases, there will be gaps between who the person is and who the person seeks to be. There's a role discontinuity (a lack of fit). Sometimes this occurs when a person moves into a new role, but normally the inner and outer person catch up if the person is suited to this new role, and a new alignment occurs. At other times, though, this gap reflects the essential split between who the person truly is and how he or she wants to appear (for example, the person who is really angry and resentful but adopts a friendly veneer to cover up an inner hurt).

Discovering Role Discrepancies

If we look only at the surface, we won't recognize this split; however, if we learn to pay more attention, we can more accurately tune into people's roles. No matter how careful a person is, cracks in the outer shell that let us see into the inner person will appear. And that's what our inner warning signal can pick up if we're in touch with it. One key to paying more attention is to remind ourselves that to a greater or lesser extent, everyone is playing a role. This role playing can be expressed in two ways:

1. *Role alignment,* which occurs when the outer role truly expresses who the person is inside or who the person can be. This is known as role authenticity, integrity, or integration.

2. *Lack of role alignment,* which occurs when a person is using a role to be someone he or she is not and cannot become. It's characterized by a lack of authenticity, integrity, and integration.

It's important to recognize this potential split. If a person does something that seems odd or out of character, pay attention. The action may mean nothing; we all sometimes step out of a role as a kind of release or a way to express a different aspect of ourselves. But sometimes the action signals a dangerous role disparity or discontinuity. Your inner intuitive powers will help you assess the situation.

If there seems to be a clear disparity in your perceptions, you need to investigate further to determine the validity of those perceptions.

Exercise 28

RECOGNIZING ROLE DISCREPANCIES

(Time: 1–2 minutes for Part 1; 10–15 minutes for Part 2)

You can use the following exercise to help you develop this awareness. Once these insights come to you automatically, you can put the exercise aside and tune in directly to your perceptions of the person.

Part 1. Paying Attention to Warning Signs
(Time: 1–2 minutes)

Accept people as they seem to be based on your initial impressions. Assume that people are generally as they present themselves and that any role discrepancies are minor or unimportant for all practical purposes. At the same time, be open and receptive to any warning signals or subsequent impressions that counteract your first impressions and suggest that things aren't quite right. By doing so, you'll be ready to look more closely or quickly reassess your first reactions if you sense that things may not be as they initially seemed. This technique will help you do this.

To pick up warning signals, remind yourself when you first see, meet, or otherwise have contact with someone that you will remain open and alert for anything that doesn't seem quite right about that person, suggesting an important role discrepancy. While you can do this at any time, it's especially important to do it when you are making an important decision about entering into a personal or business relationship with someone (planning to work for someone, hire someone, make an investment, or commit yourself to a serious relationship). At first, formally remind yourself to pay attention; after awhile, your self-reminder will become automatic and you'll be alert to anything that seems seriously out of phase.

To give yourself this suggestion, repeat something like this to yourself when you first meet a new person or just before a scheduled meeting: ". . . I want to be sure about my initial impression, since this could be an important relationship (or decision). I want to pay careful attention. I want to remain open and alert in case anything doesn't seem or feel right. I want to notice any important discrepancies or contradictions in what the person says or does. I want to pay attention to any thoughts or feelings I may have that something isn't quite right. If I get such thoughts or feelings, I will check them out."

If you wish, program yourself to see a certain image or hear a certain word to represent this feeling. For example, tell yourself that whenever you sense that something isn't quite right, you will see the image of a sly fox and see that image in your mind. Or if you are more auditory, tell yourself that you will hear the word "fox" as a warning. After a while, you will build up an association between that image or word and any feelings you have that something is wrong, and when you see the image or hear the word, you will know it's time to investigate.

Part 2. Investigating Disparities
(Time: 10–15 minutes)

However you get a warning signal, the next step is investigating it further. The following exercise is designed to help you do this.

Find a quiet place, close your eyes, and get relaxed. Focus on your breathing for about a minute to get very relaxed.

Then, imagine the person you are investigating is seated before you and you are a judge. Off to the side there is a jury. As the judge, you can ask any questions you want; the jury will decide what is believable or true or not.

Now start asking your questions and pay attention to whatever answers or images come up. Don't try to direct the answers or images yourself. Just pose your questions and let the answers come.

First, ask your questions about the person's outer image—who does he or she want to be? How does he or she want to be seen? For example, you might ask questions like:

"Who are you?"

"What do you want to do in life?"

"How do you want other people to perceive you?"

"What personality traits and characteristics do you have?"

Then listen to or observe the response. It might come in the form of a verbal response in which the person answers your question (for example, I'm a sales manager. I'm friendly. I'm involved in lots of organizations. I have many friends. I'll give you a good deal). Or it may come in the form of an image or series of images of the person involved in everyday activities.

Should you want more information, pose the question again, and again. Listen or observe.

When you feel you have a clear picture of what this person is like outwardly, imagine that a special character witness, someone who really knows this person, has come to the stand. It could be a psychologist, a family member, a friend, anyone who really knows who this person is.

Ask the witness a series of questions about this person's inner self.

"Who is this person really?"

"What is this person really like inside?"

"What are some things this person has done that don't fit his outer image?"

"Can I really trust what this person says? Is the person really sincere?"

Again, as you ask each question, listen or observe. Again, you may hear the answer in the form of verbal replies and comments. Or you may see an image or series of images about what this person is really like. And if you want more information, ask the question again; then listen and observe.

Finally, turn to the jury and ask them what they think? Do they think the person seems to be as he or she appears? Or is there a difference between who he or she is inside and who he or she claims to be?

Then listen to what the foreman of the jury says. Notice that she gets up and reads the verdict aloud. It may be: "Guilty—he's not the person he claims to be." It may be "Not guilty (or Innocent)—we think he is who he claims," or "Mistrial—we're not sure." You can then ask the jury why—why did they answer that way. Then listen to what the foreman or members of the jury say.

When you feel the jury has finished responding, you can thank and dismiss the jury. Then imagine yourself leaving the courtroom. Let go of this experience and return to the room.

Afterwards, you can write any impressions or information you have gained, and you can use these to later help you reconfirm the correctness of your intuitive impressions.

Finally, take some action based on the verdict. If the response is "guilty," this suggests a role discrepancy. If it's "mistrial," because you're not sure, do some more checking. Ask some more questions. Then, look critically at what you find out. Alternatively, if the verdict is innocent, you can feel safer in trusting this person. But if you subsequently get additional warning signs, better check again. It may be that your beliefs or other factors are clouding the accuracy of your intuitive impressions.

∎Step 3: Recognize that What You Want to Believe May Hide the Truth

If the things we want to believe about someone are untrue, this can get in the way of seeing who that person is. Often we cling to these beliefs because we feel an emotional connection to or dependency on that person or on what he or she is claiming.

We want to believe we can make lots of money in a certain scheme. We want to believe that change is just around the corner. We don't want to believe a person we love or work with has major weaknesses, for then we will lose that source of personal and emotional support.

I've seen many examples of this hanging-on process. In one case, a chief executive made repeated promises he never kept—he failed to pay commissions; he didn't make promised promotions; he moved people around to unfairly favor others—but for a long time, in each case people made excuses for him; they justified what he did; they argued angrily if someone called their attention to the truth. Why? Because they wanted to avoid acknowledging they had been following a false or fallible leader, avoid feeling they'd made a mistake, and avoid losing the knowledge and support they believed the leader had.

Moving Beyond False Beliefs to the Truth

It is important to see through these false beliefs and to recognize the difference between desired beliefs and reality. By uncovering these false beliefs, we can push past them to the truth. By doing so, we can make accurate judgments, even with minimal information.

Exercise 29

USING AN INNER DIALOGUE TO EXAMINE YOUR BELIEFS

(Time: 5–10 minutes)

The following exercise is designed to help you check out your beliefs and take off any blinders that are keeping you from seeing the truth.

This technique is actually a conversation with yourself about whether your beliefs are true. Have a sheet of paper and a pencil available if you want to take down any notes on what occurs in this conversation. To start, get relaxed as usual and close your eyes. Concentrate on your breathing until you feel very relaxed.

Now imagine two actors or voices inside you are having a debate. One is the Believer, who wants to believe. The other is the Doubter, who wants to question and make sure everything is true. You might notice an image of your Believer and Doubter emerge; if so, notice who they are, what they are like.

Then begin the dialogue. The Believer starts it off by saying what he believes. Then the Doubter raises a series of questions. These can be simple "Why?" or "How come?" questions. "Why do you think that's true?" "How come you are convinced that this incident or event happened as described?" "Why should things be as they are?" "What is the *real* reason behind her statement?" "What is being covered up?" Let whatever doubts you have come out as questions.

Then let your Believer answer and listen to what he or she says. Notice *how* he or she says it. Does your Believer sound very sure and confident or does he or she seem unsure? Does it sound as if your Believer is hiding something? Let your Doubter ask such questions as, "Do you *really* believe what you are saying?" "Are you really confident you know what's true?" And so on. Listen to what your Believer and Doubter say; you may want to write down their answers.

Keep the process going, with your Believer stating a belief or series of beliefs, your Doubter raising questions, your Believer answering them, and your Doubter raising still more questions, and so on. Keep the process going for each belief until your Doubter runs out of questions or your Believer no longer has any answers.

Then you be the judge. Remind yourself that you have set aside all prejudgments, that you have no reason to prefer one outcome over the other. Then reflect on what the Believer and Doubter have said. If you have written down anything, review what you have written before going on. Then, ask the question: "Should I believe or doubt?" Listen carefully for the answer. It may come right away. If you still aren't sure, ask yourself: "Whose arguments do I feel most drawn to?" or "Which arguments seemed more believable, more compelling?" Again notice what comes to you.

You should have your answer now, but if you still get an uncertain, unclear message, you may need to ask more questions and listen to more answers.

When you feel you have your answer, feel the process is complete, or feel you need to get more real-world information to answer your questions, say good-bye to your Believer and Doubter and return to the room.

■Tap into Reality

It's easy to be misled by outer appearances and false beliefs into overlooking disparities and the warnings of our intuition. If you fine-tune your personal antennae to pay attention to what your inner voice is saying, however, you can pick up the subtle warning signals that point to discrepancies. Then, by investigating them, you can better decide whether or not to trust that person and what you should do.

To really understand and be aware of others and make decisions about whether to trust, enter into a relationship with or work with someone, pay attention to the answers to these key questions:

1. Is the outer image the person presents generally in alignment with the inner person or are there serious discrepancies?

2. Do you have false beliefs about who the person is or what you want him or her to be that are standing in the way of really seeing who that person is?

3. What intuitive insights do you really have about this person after the outer appearances and the desired beliefs are stripped away?

Use These Techniques Regularly

While these techniques are especially useful in the early stages of a business or personal relationship or in making a decision to work with someone, they can be used at any time. This is important because, even though a person may be initially open and honest, over time the situation can change. Even after you have formed your initial impressions and feel everything is fine, stay alert to changes and warning signs. If you begin getting those little warning signals, investigate. Ask questions; examine your beliefs. It will save lots of problems and distress in the long run.

CHAPTER 11

EMPOWER YOUR MIND
Make the "Right" Decisions Every Time

*W*e make decisions all the time—sometimes with very little or no thought—and that's fine if we're deciding whether or not to turn right or left as we walk down the street, pick up this package or that while shopping, watch this or that TV program, and so forth. But when it comes to those big important decisions—such as which job to take, whether to move, whether to change careers, whether to seek a promotion—we sometimes get stuck. We may not realize that there are more possibilities than we're considering, and so we limit our choices.

■Three Steps to First-Rate Decision Making

How should you make a decision when faced with difficult choices? There are several key methods, and in each case your intuition can help you perceive your options and make the right choices:

1. Look for *opportunities and signs* that suggest a favorable result.

2. Look for ways to *expand your options* so you have more and better possibilities from which to choose.

3. Look within to *tap your feelings and tune into what you really want,* not what you think you want, feel you should want, or are swayed because someone else wants that for you.

▐Step 1: Look for Opportunities and Signs

The idea of looking for opportunities and signs is not a new one. The Roman generals looked for signs and omens before going into battle; the Chinese searched for signs and omens to determine whether a couple should marry, and similar practices exist today.

I have had positive results following these signs. For example, when I was working with a self-help jobs club, I announced that I was looking for people interested in trying out new games with an eye toward marketing them. There was limited interest. One man, Jake, with a background in product design and law responded and suggested designing a game based on finding a job. Though I had reservations about the idea, he seemed so certain about it that I decided to jump in. We became partners and developed the game called *Get a Job!* For personal reasons, Jake was forced to drop out just as we were ready to launch the project. The company we had put together dissolved, and I was left with the developed game.

Then, out of the blue, I received a call from someone about something else—from a man who had read one of my books and was thinking about an entirely different project. I knew almost nothing about him—just a few minutes of conversation on the phone—but sensing this was the opportunity I needed, I described the game, and to make a long story short, he ended up licensing it and started marketing it to all sorts of business, government, and educational organizations as well as to individuals.

What made this possible was my openness to these coincidences. For me, they were signs to go in a particular direction; not sure where they would lead initially, I followed them, led by my intuition that these were positive signs.

Following Your Signs and Opening Your Windows of Opportunity

To take advantage of the windows of opportunity that may be open to you, follow these steps:

1. *Make yourself aware of and pay attention to these signs when they appear.* For example, if you need to make a decision keep it firmly in mind and remind yourself that you are looking for clues or guidelines to help you make it.

2. *Remember that these clues and signs come in many forms.* For some, the signs come in dreams; for others, signs are more concrete—the economy or world events. Still others get their signals from what people say, including chance remarks and comments; while others respond to anomalous or unusual events. There is no one source. The point is to notice what has a resonance or congruence for you, what leads you to believe something offers a window of opportunity for you, what makes you feel intuitively that something is "right" for you, and to use those signs that have the most meaning.

3. *When you do get a strong signal, investigate it to make sure it is valid and useful.* Don't act impulsively; sometimes we tune into the wrong signal or misinterpret what seems to be a strong clue. Examine the signal in light of the other things you are experiencing and ask yourself: "Does this sign confirm other things that I am experiencing? Does it reinforce other things that might lead me to make this decision?" If the answer is yes, it is an indication that the signal is valid and that you can use it to guide you. If the answer is no, because the sign seems inconsistent with everything else you are experiencing, investigate it further.

4. *If you truly believe that a signal is valid, be ready to respond to it.*

∎Step 2: Expand Your Options

In general, you can make better decisions when you have a number of desirable alternatives from which to choose. Too many options can sometimes be confusing and can hinder decision making; too few options can make you feel stuck, especially if none of the options really appeals to you. If that is the case, you may be able to make better decisions and break through log jams by looking for new possibilities and alternatives, so that you have more and better options from which to choose, increasing your chances of choosing and getting what you want.

Brainstorming to Find Alternatives

A good way to come up with options is by brainstorming. This technique was discussed generally in Chapter 3 (to refresh your memory about how brainstorming works, see pages 27-50). Here the focus is on how to apply brainstorming to decision making. Brainstorming is an ideal way to come up with new ideas because it helps you create alternatives. Alternatives aren't helpful when you are in an either-or situation in which you have no input; but where options are possible, creative brainstorming can help you make better decisions.

Exercise 30 _____

CREATING INNER FOCUS FOR BETTER BRAINSTORMING

(Time: 5–10 minutes)

The following exercise will help you to focus so that you can brainstorm ideas and alternatives most effectively. Initially, do it when you are alone and in a quiet place. With practice, you can achieve this state anywhere (this exercise will help you tune out external influences).

Get in a calm, relaxed state with your eyes closed. Concentrate on focusing inward. Imagine that you are looking at something with a point in its center, such as a long deep hole, a tunnel, or a bulls-eye. As you gaze at it, project yourself into that central point. You feel totally directed, totally focused. That point is the only thing that exists in your consciousness.

Then, with your consciousness directed on that point, notice how you can turn the stimuli of the outer world on and off. To do this, continue focusing on this point; then notice whatever sounds, smells, movements, or other sensations are around you. Pay attention to them for a moment.

Next, turn your attention completely away, back to that center point. Again imagine that nothing else exists and turn off those external sounds, smells, movements, or other sensations.

Then turn your attention back to the external world for a few minutes; then back to your inner world. Do this several times. Notice that you have the ability to shift your attention back and forth; you can be totally focused either outside or in, as you choose.

Next concentrate on holding your attention somewhere in the middle; you are aware of both your internal world and the external world. It's as if your awareness is on a fence, and you can shift your focus from one side to the other or sit right on the fence so you can experience both worlds simultaneously. Practice shifting your focus from one place to another—to the external world, to the middle area between worlds, and to the internal world. Try moving gradually from world to world with a stop in the middle; then practice jumping your attention back and forth between the external and internal world. As you do, notice how your awareness and experience change and notice that it becomes easier and easier to shift your focus.

Now redirect your focus back to that center point and gradually release your attention. When you feel ready, return to the everyday world and open your eyes.

Exercise 31

GENERATING DECISION-MAKING IDEAS

(Time: 5–10 minutes)

Individual (personal) brainstorming is the method most often used for decision making. At the initial idea-generating stage you should:

1. Get into a receptive, responsive, inward-looking state of mind.

2. Let go of the logical-rational-critical-judgmental part of your mind.

3. Find a quiet, calm, relaxing place in which you can tune out the influences of the external world.

4. Once in this receptive state, ask a triggering question. Be specific, but present your question in an open-ended way, such as: "In how many ways can I solve this *particular* problem?"

5. After you present your question, remain centered, focused, and receptive. Let the ideas flow up and through you. Pay attention, but just observe or listen; don't try to guide or direct. At this stage, accept whatever comes.

6. Record the responses so you don't lose them; write them down or record them on tape. In some cases, as you write or record, you may receive additional ideas. Don't inhibit them, just let them happen, if they occur.

7. Keep the process going as long as you are readily coming up with ideas. When the ideas start slowing down, ask yourself "Is there anything else?" or ask a related question. Listen or observe to see if there are further ideas.

Then, when you feel the process is complete, let go of this concentrated, focused inward state and return to a more neutral or logical-rational state. Now, for the next stage, use your logical-rational-critical-judgmental mind to review and assess the ideas you have come up with. One good way is to rate the ideas on a scale of 0 to 5 to choose those you like the best and then prioritize or choose the best one to make a selection of alternatives. You can use the chart in Chapter 3 (page 41).

■Step 3: Tap into Your Feelings and Tune into Your Real Desires

While expanding your options and alternatives can give you more choices when a limited selection is the problem, what do you do when you know the possibilities and you can't decide among them? Or what if your choices are limited to "yes," "no," or "maybe"? What if you don't have the time to get more information or work out the pros and cons logically? What if you find that additional information is just further confusing you and weighing you down?

One way to break through the confusion, figure out what you really want and make a quick decision is to tune into your inner mind to learn what your unconscious desires are or what your intuition thinks is best for you. Your intuition, once you access it, can help you decide; it can break through the self-imposed barriers—fear statements such as "It won't work," and "I can't do it"—which you put up in the way when faced with a difficult decision.

The techniques in this chapter are designed to make you more sensitive to that inner voice or vision.

Pathways to Your Inner Feelings

It is important to realize that when you tune into your intuition to determine what you really want to do, you can use many channels or pathways to access it. The key is to find those intuitive mechanisms that work best for you. As previously discussed, the four ways you may get intuitive information include: seeing, hearing, feeling, and sensing that you know something. The different channels or pathways through which this information may come include:

➤ automatic writing;

➤ automatic drawing;

➤ mental journeys;

➤ "yes," "no," "maybe" signals from your intuitive mind;

➤ physical signals from your body.

Each person uses each of these pathways a little differently. One person may go on a mental journey by imagining him or herself going into a dark room and seeing the answer appear in the form of a film on the screen; another may go into a workshop and see the answer on a computer monitor; still another may go on a long mental journey into the mountains and seek the answer from a wise old man; and some may use more traditional shamanic imagery from tribal peoples. Similarly, there are a variety of ways to use automatic writing, to receive impulses from your brain and signals from your body.

Different people prefer different techniques, and many people use multiple approaches, depending on how they feel. The idea is to use the approach or approaches that work best for you. Experiment with different methods until you find those you prefer.

The following exercises demonstrate how you can use these techniques to tap into your own intuitive unconscious to make a decision. Incidentally, although the focus of this chapter has been on decision making and problem solving, these techniques can readily be applied to many other situations as well, such as developing ideas for new projects.

Exercise 32

AUTOMATIC WRITING—A DECISION-MAKING TOOL[1]

(Time: 5–15 minutes)

Automatic writing can help you get the insights you need to make the right decision or find the answer to a problem or question. While any form of writing—longhand, typewriter or computer—is fine, when you are just starting you may find that longhand is more conducive to the process (you can go off to a quiet, isolated place where you may feel a more direct connection with your thoughts).

To set the stage, create a comfortable writing environment that will help you get into a quiet, inner-focused state. You may want to dim the lights, light a candle, or put on some soft background music. Have your writing materials readily available.

When you're ready to begin, get calm and relaxed, using a relaxation technique or even a repetitive physical exercise to get you into a trancelike state. Once in this relaxed, focused, receptive state, you are ready to begin writing. If you have music on, turn it off so you can concentrate.

Now begin asking any questions about your decision. Be receptive to whatever comes, and immediately begin writing whatever comes to mind. You can ask your question however you wish: "What would I really like to do?" "Where should I go?" "What are my alternatives; which one do I really prefer?" "Which choice will be of the most benefit to me?"

Then write right away and write as quickly as possible. Even if the words don't make sense or come in single words or phrases, rather than in sentences, write them down. Don't think or analyze. You may find that you sometimes get thoughts; you should write them down as if you were a reporter. Or the writing may become a direct line between

---

[1] The techniques in this section are adapted from *Mind Power*.

your thoughts and the paper. You don't even hear your self-talk; instead you discover what you are thinking as you write or after the words are written. This latter state is ideal, because your automatic writing is then directly recording your inner consciousness. Sometimes, particularly when you are in this deeply focused state, you may feel the thoughts are coming to you from a spirit or guide, and that's fine, too. Whatever helps you access your inner truth will contribute to the process.

However you get your answers, just keep writing. When you have finished writing the answer to one question, ask another. Keep asking questions and writing the answers until the questions and responses stop and you feel the process is complete.

Then let go of this inner state and come back to ordinary consciousness. Review what you have written and interpret any words or phrases that are not immediately clear. What you have written should indicate the choice you want to make.

Exercise 33

AUTOMATIC DRAWING—PICTURE YOUR DECISION

(Time: 5–15 minutes)

If you are better able to tap your intuitive mind through images and symbols than through words and thoughts, you may prefer automatic drawing to writing. The steps are much the same. Instead of writing down your answers you will draw pictures and images, and then interpret these images.

The steps are the same as for automatic writing. Set the stage by creating a comfortable environment. Have the drawing materials readily available. These can be very simple materials—paper or a notebook, and pencil or pen or, if you prefer, special drawing materials—sketch paper, crayons, colored pencils, and magic markers, and so on.

When you're ready to begin, as earlier, get calm and relaxed, using the same techniques described for automatic writing.

Then ask questions about your decision and be receptive to whatever comes.

Begin drawing right away and draw as quickly as possible. The images may come in various forms—complete pictures, symbols, sometimes even words. Just draw whatever you see and don't think or analyze.

You may find that sometimes you are seeing pictures and drawing what you have seen after the fact. Or the drawing may become like a direct line for your thoughts—you see the images only as you are drawing them or after you have drawn them. The ideal is to seek this latter state, because then your automatic drawing is directly recording your inner consciousness and you are more fully in this focused, concentrated inner state. Sometimes, particularly when you are in this deeply focused state, you may feel the images are coming to you from a spirit or guide, and that's fine, too. Whatever helps you feel you are accessing your inner truth will contribute to the process.

However you get your answers, just keep drawing. When you have finished drawing the answer to one question, ask another. Keep asking questions and drawing what you see, until the questions and responses stop and you feel complete with the process.

Let go of this inner state and come back to ordinary consciousness. Review what you have drawn and interpret any symbols or images that are unclear. Whatever you have drawn should indicate the choice you want to make.

Exercise 34 _____

MENTAL JOURNEYS TO REACH DECISIONS

(Time: 5–15 minutes for each technique)

Mental journeys can take a variety of forms. In general, they involve taking a mental trip to a place where you will find the answer to your question. The journey itself helps you get into this deeper, focused, aware state. Once you arrive, the particular place you go or the person or guide or things you encounter there can help you find the answer. Each person's journey is personal; use whatever images and interpretations of these images that work for you. The key is to get in touch with your inner knowledge, in whatever way works best for you. Here are two representative types of mental journeys; use these or feel free to create your own.

Technique 1: Asking a Counselor for Advice[2]

This technique takes you to a workshop where you'll speak with an expert adviser or counselor who will know all the answers you need

---

2 This technique is adapted from the technique described in *Mind Power*.

to know. Depending on your preference, this guide will appear in person or on a computer screen.

Begin by getting relaxed; close your eyes. Imagine a special workshop or office in your house where you can go to find out whatever you want to know. It can be a special room anyplace in your house. Perhaps it is in the basement, attic, or garage. It might even be a special building on the roof or in the backyard.

Now, wherever it is, imagine your walk to go there. Go slowly and leisurely, so you will be ready to go to work when you arrive. As you walk, notice what is around you. When you come to the door to this room, open it and go inside. As you enter, look around. There are all kinds of things there that you have been working on. There may be books and papers or things you have made or projects you are working on.

Now sit down in the room. If you want to get your answer from an expert, just wait, and he or she will come. Or if you prefer, you can turn on an imaginary computer console. Now call on this expert to help you. In a moment, this expert will appear in person, or the screen will light up with a communication from this expert. Notice what the expert is like and say a few words of welcome. The expert may be someone you know, someone in the field you want help with, or he or she may just be someone who is very wise and knowledgeable.

Then state the question or problem you need to make a decision about; ask for help in deciding among the alternatives. Listen as your counselor or adviser tells you what to do. He or she may tell you verbally, or the answer may appear on the computer screen.

If you have more questions, ask them and your counselor will reply. Again, wait for your answer. When you have no more questions, tell your counselor you are done, and your counselor will say goodbye and leave.

Then turn off the computer if you used one and leave your workshop. Return to your house, and as you do, return to normal consciousness. Open your eyes.

Usually, this process provides clear answers. If, however, your counselor has not provided answers or has asked you to wait, this probably means you don't have enough information or that the situation is still unclear. If this is the case, wait a few days and ask your questions again; or try some of the other empowered mind techniques to obtain more information. You may also need to get more information from external sources (such as other people, magazines, or books) about the situation to help you make your decision.

Technique 2: Taking a Shamanic Journey to Find the Answer

This technique takes you to a distant setting to get your answer. It can take you anyplace, but some typical trips are to the top of a mountain to learn the answers from a wise old man or woman, to a pool of water where you will see the answer in the water, to a cave where you will meet power animals or teachers who can help you, to the clouds where you will encounter wise teachers or spiritual beings, and so forth. The following exercise is designed to let you choose where you want to go and whom you want to meet when you get there to help you make your decision.

You can use this technique in one of two ways: One is to read this description and use it to guide your experience in a general way. The other is to record the journey on tape and play it back while you listen.

Begin by getting relaxed. Close your eyes. Then, imagine yourself in the middle of a meadow. It is a beautiful sunny day and you are sitting under a shady tree.

Now look around the meadow to decide where you want to go for help with your decision. If you look to the west, you can take a path down to the river or a lake. If you look to the north, you can follow a path that leads to a cave. If you look to the east, you can follow a path to a mountain, and you can walk up to the top of it. If you look to the south, you will see a very tall tree that leads up into the clouds, and, if you wish, you can climb the tree to the clouds. Wherever you go, you will feel very comfortable and very safe, and you will find your answers there.

Now, choose which path you want to follow—to the river or a lake; to the cave; to the mountain top; or to the clouds. Begin walking. As you do, notice the scenery around you. You may notice lush green foliage, or you may see flowers. You may hear birds singing. You may see some animals in the distance. Just notice whatever's there and feel comfortable and at ease as you walk on this beautiful day, where the air is clear and warmed by the sun.

Now you are approaching your destination. If you are going to the water or the cave, notice the path is descending now. Or if you are going to the mountain or up the tree to the clouds, notice the path is going up. Now see your destination, and continue your walk.

Once you are there, look around. You may see someone approach who will be your teacher or guide. Or you may see an animal who has come to help you, your power animal. Whoever approaches—person or animal—ask if he or she will be your teacher or guide or will show you to your teacher or guide.

Your teacher will welcome you and invite you to ask a question. Do so and then listen or observe. You will get your answer. It may be in the form of words; or your teacher may take you somewhere, show you something, or ask you to look ahead of you to a place where you will see your answer revealed. Just be open and receptive to whatever comes, in whatever form.

If you have additional questions, you can ask them after you get the answer to your first question.

Afterwards, thank your teacher, who will lead you to the entrance. Say good-bye. You will see the path you took; return on it now. Go back to the meadow to the tree from which you began your journey. Sit down under the tree again, and gradually let go of the experience and return to your everyday consciousness.

Making Quick Decisions

For quick, everyday decisions, you obviously can't take the long amount of time needed to go on mental journeys or have an ongoing dialogue with your expert. Instead, you need a way to tap into your intuition quickly, to get a rapid-fire answer to a question that needs only a simple yes, no, or maybe (not sure or find out more). If there are just a few alternatives, you want a quick signal to say this or that is best.

This approach is particularly useful when you have to make a fast go-no go decision or if you are feeling outside pressure to make a decision but feel some inner resistance. A quick intuitive response can help you make the choice and feel better about your decision.

The following techniques are designed to provide you with some alternate ways of getting quick answers from your intuitive mind in the form of words, images, or symbols, or from your body.

Exercise 35

YES, NO, OR MAYBE—QUICK ANSWERS FROM YOUR INTUITIVE MIND

(Time: 10–15 minutes)

This technique, which uses words, images, or symbols, is designed to quickly tap into your inner intuition or feelings to get an immediate and clear "yes," "no," or "not sure."

To use this technique effectively, you either have to do some preliminary conditioning to get your mental screen ready to respond immediately[3] or you can look within to see what word, image, or symbol you used in similar situations and use it.

To get in touch with the feeling or sense you have when you must give a yes or no answer or make a quick, clear choice, take some time to get relaxed and comfortable and close your eyes. Then, in this very relaxed, comfortable state, imagine you are going to be taking a truth test in which you want to see your real feelings. Now ask yourself a series of questions to which you know the answer and can answer yes or no or you can make a clear either/or choice: such as: "Was I born in California?" "Did I go to school in New York?" "Is my favorite color red or blue?"

As you give each truthful answer, notice how you feel. Also, notice if you gave the answer as a word you heard, as a word you said in your mind, or as an image you saw or something you *felt.*

Now ask either those same questions or different questions, but this time answer untruthfully. Intentionally say no or make the wrong choice. Again, notice the feelings, images, and so forth associated with saying no.

Reflect on the differences in how you felt. You will probably find that your answers when you were saying something you really felt were much clearer and stronger; you had a sense of certainty; perhaps the image of the word seemed brighter or the sound of the word in your mind seemed louder.

---

3 This discussion of conditioning is adapted from *Mind Power*.

Now ask yourself a series of questions to which you don't have answers or about which you haven't yet made a decision. Ask your intuitive mind to give you the appropriate response. At first, each time you respond, notice the feelings, images, and associations you experience with that yes, no, or choice. Get a clear sense of what it is like to say yes, no, or to make a choice and be very firm in that decision.

Then speed up the process. Ask the questions faster and faster and give a quicker and quicker response. Don't pay conscious attention to the feelings, images, and so on, associated with the act of saying yes, no, or making a choice. The goal is to respond so automatically, so intuitively, you don't have to think about your response anymore. Your feelings, images, and associations are all triggered at once as you respond, and you know immediately how you really feel on that gut or inner level.

Finally, when you feel ready, stop asking questions and responding and return to the room.

Continue to practice this technique for about a week, until you feel that your yes-no-quick choice response has become a part of your life. Also, try using it to get answers in everyday life. You'll find your answers will come more and more quickly and easily in whatever form they appear.

Exercise 36

PHYSICAL CLUES—QUICK ANSWERS FROM YOUR BODY

(Time: 3–5 minutes)

An alternate way to get yes, no, or not sure answers is by asking your body. In this way, you go past your conscious thoughts to your inner feelings, which are reflected in how your body reacts.

As with the previous technique to tune into your intuitive mind, you need some practice to train your responses until they become automatic. The difference here is that you are training your physical body rather than your mind to respond with cues. After you work with these physical movements, you can visualize them or replace them with a voice in your mind, so you can pick up these cues anywhere.

The following technique involves using your arm as a pendulum; you can use another part or your whole body if you prefer.[4]

To begin, place your elbow on a desk and hold your arm and hand up. Then, move it around freely in all directions. Next, imagine that your arm is a truth meter. Sway your arm like a pendulum backward and forward, and as you do, repeat the words: "yes . . . yes" to yourself again and again. This backward and forward motion means "yes." Next, sway your arm to the right and left, and as you do, repeat the word: "no . . . no" to yourself again and again. This right to left and left to right motion means "no." Finally, sway your arm in the free motion you started with. As you do, repeat the phrase: "not sure" or "maybe" to yourself. Choose the phrase you prefer and repeat it again and again. This free-form motion means "not sure" or "maybe."

To test that you have made the associations between "yes" "no" and "not sure (or maybe)" and your arm's motions, try asking a few yes-no questions to which you know the answers. Your arm should respond with the appropriate swaying motions. Once it does this consistently, you are ready to begin asking it for answers.

As you become more practiced in using this technique, so the bodily motions are truly automatic, you don't actually need to move your arm. You can imagine this movement in your mind's eye. Just ask your question and observe how your arm responds to get your answer. Later, you won't even need to imagine your arm in motion. You can just ask your question, and you will feel your body respond with a yes or no.

Some Tips on Asking Your Questions

In both these techniques, it's important to ask your questions in the right way so you tap into what you really feel. For example, don't ask "What *should* I do?" because that implies outside pressure influencing your decision. Instead, ask your question in a more neutral or feeling way; for example, "Which do I really *feel* best about doing?" or "Which do I personally prefer?"

---

4 This exercise is adapted from *Mind Power*.

If you get a lot of "not sure's" or "maybe's" to a question, it may be that you need more information, in which case, ask your question at a later time. Or it may be because you are not asking the question clearly or because outside influences or your beliefs about what you *should* do or think are getting in the way. To find out, ask: "Is my question unclear?" "Is someone else influencing my answer?" "Are my beliefs or thoughts getting in the way?" If this is the case, clarify or reframe your question, or push your conscious thoughts and feelings aside so you can listen to your inner self.

CHAPTER 12

EMPOWER YOUR MIND

Unleash Creativity and Innovation

Creativity is an essential part of human nature—a kind of evolutionary key—that has enabled humans to thrive. Our environment is always changing, and our creativity helps us respond to or influence that change. Creativity allows us to constantly remake ourselves and remodel our behavior to best fit the new conditions or sometimes shape those new conditions.

Today's technological revolution is a good example. It has transformed the way many of us live and work and has changed life's pace. Most people have had to adapt to these changes to one degree or another.

■The Power of Creativity and Innovation

Your inner creativity can help you respond successfully to change. It can be a wellspring of a variety of new ideas that you can use to:

➤ be more efficient and productive;

➤ create new useful and profitable products or businesses;

➤ design better policies and procedures under which any type of offices or groups can function;

➤ provide more and better leadership and direction;

➤ reshape yourself and what you do to open doors to new opportunities;

➤ feel more power and self-confidence so you can do more;

➤ make life more interesting and exciting for yourself and the important others in your life.

∎Creativity and Change

Often there is great resistance to change because people are afraid of where it will lead. They fear it may be dangerous—and certainly, change can be—particularly if it is unanticipated or out of control.

But when you are receptive and view change in a positive, productive way, you discover how many possibilities change offers and how much you can gain from change.

How good are you at recognizing or anticipating changes in your life? Are there major changes you are experiencing now or that you anticipate in the near future? Are there any things you should change in what you are doing? Use the exercise and chart on page 184 to note changes and what you might do to respond.

Exercise 37 _____

RECOGNIZING AND RESPONDING TO CHANGE

(Time: 5–10 minutes)

Get comfortable and relaxed. Then use any of the previously described techniques for finding answers to questions, and ask yourself the following questions. Listen for the answers, and write them down.

➤ "What major changes have recently occurred in my life? In my work? In my relationships?"

➤ "What have I done to respond to them?"

➤ "How well do I feel I responded?" (Rate your responses from 0 to 5.)

➤ "What should I do now, if anything, to respond to these changes?"

➤ "What major changes do I anticipate occurring in the next 3 to 6 months that will affect me? In my work? In my relationships?"

➤ "What can I do to respond to these changes?"

➤ "What major changes do I anticipate occurring in the next six months to a year that will affect me? In my work? In my relationships?"

➤ "What can I do to respond to these changes?"

After you have finished answering your questions, let go and return to your normal state. Review your answers and consider which of these responses you want to implement now.

Creative Repackaging: How to Present the New You

This review of the changes that have affected or will affect you and how you can change may lead you to realize you need to present yourself in new ways to adjust to new times. In turn, this revamped look may be just what's needed to convince others you can do something new or different. By presenting yourself in a new way, you change the way people view you, and you change their perceptions of what you can do. It signifies that you are ready and able to respond to change.

This is what happened to Bill, a lawyer specializing in immigration. He had done very well, but, after twelve years doing immigration law, he felt burned out. His background was certainly impressive, but specialized, and those hiring in other related fields, from law to business and nonprofit management, couldn't see past his highly developed but specialized skills. For Bill, creativity meant thinking of new ways to present himself. He looked at the skills he had as an immigration lawyer and the results he had achieved in using skills rather than at the particular tasks he had done. As a result, he repackaged himself as a problem solver and operational development specialist. He stopped using the term

RECOGNIZING CHANGES AND HOW I CAN RESPOND TO THEM

Current Changes	How I Responded	Ratings (Scale 0–5)	What Should I Do Now?
Major recent changes	What did I do?		
In work:			
In relationships:			

Anticipated Changes	How I Can Respond	Ratings (Scale 0–5)	What Else Can I Do?
In next 3–6 months	What can I do?		
In work:			
In relationships?			
In next six months to one year	What can I do?		
In work:			
In relationships?			

lawyer or attorney to describe himself, though that is what he had been for over a dozen years. By creatively repackaging himself, he not only saw himself in a new way but he created a new prism through which prospective employers could regard him. Within several weeks he found a new job helping managers troubleshoot and resolve the problems in their organization.

∎The Three Keys to Creativity

Creativity does more than help you adapt effectively to change. It can lead to many other desired results. And while we often think of creativity in terms of results, results are only the end product.

Being creative is a process of responding in new ways. It can be harnessed to do everything, from creating different forms of artistic expression to reshaping yourself, your relationships, your work environment, and society as a whole. Underlying this creativity is a readiness to respond, a willingness to try, an openness to new things, and a lack of fear of change. Combined with an awareness of what needs fixing or changing, you can apply these techniques to come up with new ideas for just about anything. Three basic elements are all you need:

1. *The ability to perceive and think in innovative ways:* an approach that helps you come up with new ideas, using techniques such as brainstorming and intuition to envision alternatives.

2. *An openness to alternative approaches:* so you're willing to accept new ideas and act on them.

3. *The insight to identify areas in which creative responses are needed:* giving you the ability to perceive which changes are necessary or desirable and which aren't.

These three elements represent a creative approach to life that can be applied to anything. If you learn to incorporate a creative approach to whatever you do, you can call on your creative force at any time and for a wide variety of purposes. Creativity becomes part of who you are—a natural way of being—so you are always ready to use it.

∎Say Yes to New Ideas

Sometimes our creativity is blocked because we are afraid of new ideas or of making changes. This fear can also prevent us from recognizing where a new idea or a change is needed. For each new invention, you can find people who were happy with the old idea, resisted the new, and were subsequently left behind—the silent movie producers who rejected the coming of sound; the decision makers at Hewlett-Packard who didn't see any sense in the personal computer idea of some employees who left to found Apple; the resistance of IBM executives to the software system ideas of Ross Perot who made his billions from them: These are but a few examples.

Fear and resistance in our day-to-day lives can also be roadblocks. The following exercises will help you to identify and overcome any fears and resistances you might have.

Overcoming Resistance or Fear

These techniques are designed to help you look within to discover either a general nay-saying attitude or a specific fear about a particular situation that is holding you back. The first exercise is concerned with your attitude generally; the second is intended to help with a particular fear or situation.

Exercise 38

OVERCOMING A NEGATIVE ATTITUDE

(Time: 7–15 minutes)

As usual, get comfortable and relaxed. Close your eyes. Focus on your breathing for a minute or so until you feel very centered and relaxed.

Now take a mental journey to wherever you want to go to get inner information—a quiet calm place, a room where you can meet your inner expert—and ask yourself a series of questions to see if you are afraid of or resistant to new things or to some specific things. Then, as you ask each question, don't try to answer it with your conscious mind. Instead, just listen or observe and wait for the answer to come to you.

Ask your first question and listen to the answer: "How do I feel about new ideas? Do I like things that are new or different?"

Next ask and again listen: "How do I usually react when I experience something new and different?" Ask to see a few examples—they can be situations at work or in your personal life. Take a few minutes to look at these situations.

Notice what comes up. Have you usually been receptive? If you have been receptive, just compliment yourself for being open and remind yourself that you will continue to be so in the future. Then gradually bring yourself back to normal consciousness and return to the room.

Or if you are normally not receptive, ask yourself, "Why not? What fears are standing in the way? Why am I apt to say no? Why am I holding back from being open to change?" Notice the answers. Now, if you feel ready to rid yourself of these fears, imagine that you are collecting these fears together. Imagine that each of these fears is an object, and you are picking them up one by one to get rid of them. You can burn them, bury them, throw them in the river, bomb them. However you want to do it, just see these fears disappearing. As each one disappears, you feel freer and freer. You feel more open and receptive; more ready to see new ideas without criticizing or prejudging or thinking them wrong in advance. In fact, you are eager now to learn about new ideas and to try them out; your fear of doing so is gone; you feel ready to do and discover new things.

Then, holding that feeling of interest and excitement, tell yourself that "In the future, I will be more open and receptive. I will be more ready to hear about and act on new things. And if I feel myself resisting and holding back, I will tell myself 'No. Don't say no. Be open. Be ready to wait and see.'"

Repeat this reminder to yourself several times, while feeling this sense of interest and excitement. Then, let go of this experience, leave the place you have gone to get information, and return to your everyday consciousness.

Exercise 39

OVERCOMING A SPECIFIC FEAR

(Time: 7–15 minutes)

As usual, get comfortable and relaxed. Close your eyes. Again, focus on your breathing for a minute or so until you feel very centered and relaxed.

Now, take a mental journey wherever you want to go to get inner information—a quiet calm place, a room where you can meet your inner expert—and ask yourself a series of questions to see if you are afraid of or resistant to some new idea or situation. As you ask each question, don't try consciously to answer it. Instead, just listen or observe and wait for the answer to come to you.

Ask your first question and listen to the answer: "Why do I fear this new idea or change or particular situation (describe it)? What do I see holding me back?"

Then listen to the answer. Are you afraid of a person? Is it something you have to do that bothers you? Are you afraid of being wrong? Of coming up with ideas that aren't good?

Reflect on what has come to you. If you feel ready to get rid of these fears yourself, imagine that you are collecting them. Imagine that each of these fears is like an object or painting, and you are picking them up one by one to get rid of them. You can burn them, bury them, throw them in the river, bomb them. However you want to do it, just see these fears disappearing. As each one disappears, you feel freer and freer. You feel more open and receptive; you are more ready to approach this situation in a new way; you are ready to think of new ideas without criticizing or prejudging or thinking them wrong in advance. In fact, you are now eager to tackle this idea or situation; your fear of doing so is gone.

Holding that feeling of interest and excitement, tell yourself, "I am ready and eager to deal with this situation now. I will be more ready to hear about and act on these new ideas. If I feel myself beginning to resist or hold back, I will tell myself 'No. Don't say no. Be open. Be ready to consider and try out this new idea or situation. There's nothing to be concerned about or afraid of. I'll think of the possibilities and know it will be possible. I'll say yes to these possibilities. I'll say yes to these possibilities.'"

Repeat this reminder several times, while feeling this sense of interest and excitement. Then let go of this experience and return to your everyday consciousness.

Exercise 40

IDENTIFYING WHAT NEEDS CHANGING

(Time: 7–15 minutes)

In what areas do you need new ideas? What would you like to change? The following technique is designed to help you consider what you feel needs changing and to help you set priorities for what you want to focus on changing. Then, you can either brainstorm or use your intuition to seek new ideas and help you select among alternatives. Have a paper and pencil ready and copy the chart on page 190 to list the areas where new ideas or changes are needed.

To begin, get comfortable and relaxed. Close your eyes. Focus on your breathing to get into this centered state.

Now take a mental journey to wherever you want to go to get inner information—a quiet, calm place, a room where you can meet your inner expert—and ask yourself this question: "What new things or changes would I like to see in my life?" List whatever comes.

If you are interested in making changes in a particular area, such as at work, at home, in a certain relationship, ask about that: "What new things or changes would I like to see in (fill in the topic)." Again, list whatever comes.

Finally, ask, "Are there any other new things or changes I would like to make?" And again list whatever comes.

After you've listed all you can think of, let go of the experience and return to your everyday consciousness.

Review the list you have created, and rate the areas on a rating system of 0 (no interest) to 3 (high interest) to prioritize and select the area (or few areas) on which you want to focus first. If there are more than a few high-priority areas, go back to those and rate your priorities within this group. Once you have set your priorities, you can focus on applying idea-generating techniques to these areas.

IDENTIFYING WHERE CHANGES ARE NEEDED

Suggested Areas for Change	*Rating (Scale 0–3)*

■Four Ways to Use Your Creativity to Generate Ideas

Just like any skill, the ability to be creative—the ability to come up with new ideas and apply them in an open, receptive way—can be developed through practice. Just as you can get better at writing, speaking, or anything by doing it, so you can become more creative by taking the time to work on coming up with and using new ideas. The more you do it, the easier it gets, since you are in effect exercising your creative muscle, getting more in touch with the intuitive idea-generating part of your mind. Whatever the arena, you will find you have more ideas.

The following methods are particularly valuable in the work place, but you can easily adapt them to come up with ideas in all areas of your life. The exercises will help you develop your creative abilities generally as well as provide some specific techniques you can apply in everyday work and personal situations. You can use any of these techniques alone, or try brainstorming with a friend or in a group.

Method 1: New Ways to Use What You Have

If you already have something, and think of new ways to use it, you can:

➤ increase its value to yourself and others;

➤ save money;

➤ expand its potential market.

The concept can be applied to people (finding new tasks for present employees); products (turning a pile of stones into "Pet Rocks"); places (turning something on one's property into a tourist attraction); just about anything. It's a simple but useful concept that allows you to stretch your resources as far as they go.

The following exercise will help you focus on new uses for "old" things. You'll begin by thinking about new uses for things generally just to get the process going; then, you'll think of a situation in which you would like to find new ways to use something and apply the technique to that.[1]

Exercise 41 _____

NEW USES FOR FAMILIAR THINGS

(Time: 10–15 minutes)

You'll start with something that's familiar. Then, see how many new and different uses you can come up with for it. Copy the chart on page 193 to record your ideas. The exercise is divided into two parts: Part 1 is a practice warm-up to get your ideas flowing, and Part 2 applies the process to a real situation.

Part 1: The Practice Warm Up

To get your creative juices flowing, choose the first common objects that come to mind—things in your office, home, outside on the street, or natural objects. Make a list of these objects and pick five to ten you want to work on. For each of these objects, list as many ways as you can think of to use it. For example: What are all the things you can do with a glass? A light bulb? A box? A leaf? A piece of paper and a mirror? Feel free to come up with novel, unusual, even outrageous uses. Feel free to change the object's size, shape, or color or to use two or more objects together in new ways.

Part 2: Applying the Process

When you feel warmed up, think of something at work or in your personal life to which you want to apply this technique. For example:

➤ new uses for products in your product line;

➤ new ways to use your computer;

➤ new tasks your work group can do;

➤ new no-cost activities you can do at home with your family.

Now think about other ways or things to which you might apply this technique. Later, you can actually do so.

_____

[1] Adapted from *Mind Power*, p. 78.

NEW USES FOR FAMILIAR THINGS

Familiar Object	*New Uses*

Method 2: New Paths to Your Goal

There are many paths to any goal—whether it's a career goal, such as receiving a promotion, or an accomplishment, such as publishing a book, or a personal goal, such as taking that trip to Australia. Sometimes a clear path leads to your goal or you already have what you need to get there. At other times, the path isn't clear or you're missing something that will get you there, and that's when your creativity can help you find the way or the skills and resources needed to reach your goal. As in a maze, different approaches can be used to create the path to your goal. By accessing your creativity you'll come up with a variety of approaches, and you can choose the one or ones you want to try.

The following exercise will help you focus on finding new paths to a chosen goal. These paths can be new strategies and procedures or new materials and resources—whatever is needed to get there.

Exercise 42 _____

FINDING NEW PATHS TO A GOAL

(Time: 10–15 minutes)

In this exercise, you start with a goal you want to achieve or a need you want to satisfy. Then see how many ways you can achieve it. Have some paper and pencil handy to write down ideas or copy the chart on page 195. The exercise is divided into two parts: Part 1 is a warm-up to get your ideas flowing, and part 2 applies the process to a real situation.

Part 1: The Practice Warm-Up

Think of any goal or need. It can be something work-related or personal. It doesn't have to be real. Then brainstorm all the ways you can get there. Write them down. Consider both the different methods and resources you will need to get there.

Part 2: Applying the Process

Think of a real goal or need you have right now. This can be personal or work-related. Then brainstorm all the ways you can to achieve this goal and write them down. Consider both the different methods and resources you will need to get there. When you've come up with all the ideas you can, review them and choose those you can actually implement.

FINDING NEW PATHS TO A GOAL

The Goal(s) I Want to Achieve	*New Ways to Achieve that Goal*

Method 3: New Ways to Make Changes

Making changes is very basic to our society. Change is the basis of technological and social progress—making changes in the way things are and combining what exists in new ways. Just think of the many positive words in our language that express the high value we place on the benefits of creative change: new, better, improved, faster, more efficient, more effective, cheaper, more attractive, more exciting...You can undoubtedly continue the list yourself. The point is that all sorts of things can be changed by altering different elements or making new connections and combinations.

So what would you like to change? The following technique is designed to get you thinking about making changes, new connections, and new combinations.

Exercise 43 _____

MAKING CHANGES[2]

(Time: 7–10 minutes for each part)

The following exercises will give you practice in changing things and trying out new combinations and connections. Use the practice exercises to limber up; then apply these techniques to specific things you want to change. Have a piece of paper and a pencil handy or copy the chart on page 199.

Technique 1: Objects

This exercise is especially useful when applied to changing material things; for example, creating new inventions, improving technology, developing new product ideas.

For practice, start by making a list of familiar objects. Look around your room, outside your window, or just write down whatever comes to mind. Then think of all the ways you can change that object. Think about its size, its color, its style, its construction, its materials, its shape, and so forth. Just brainstorm and list any changes you think of.

---

[2] Adapted from *Mind Power*, pp. 81–83.

As you mentally make changes in the physical qualities of that object, imagine what it might be used for in its new form. Feel free to think of either practical or fanciful applications. Later, review the ideas to see if any of them might have practical applications. For now you are just exercising your creative idea-generating abilities. (For example, say you change the *size* of a rubber ball. A small ball might be for throwing or bouncing, a giant ball might be used for crushing an object. Or say you change the materials the ball is made of. A very hard substance might be a cannon ball; a very soft material might be a child's toy.)

Now apply this technique to some object you really do want to change—such as to create a new or better product.

Technique 2: Places

This exercise is especially useful if you want to change your physical environment.

For practice, look at a picture or at the scene around you. How many changes can you make? Imagine that you are superimposing another picture over the first and imagine yourself making the changes on this picture. In effect, you are simultaneously looking at or looking back and forth between two scenes—the one that exists and the picture you are changing in your mind's eye. As you look at these two scenes, make any of the following changes:

➤ *Add* additional things or people into the scene.

➤ *Take away* something or someone.

➤ *Rearrange* the things or people.

➤ *Change the size relationships* of the things or people.

➤ *Try a combination of these changes.*

Don't worry about making useful changes; you are just practicing. If anything useful comes out of this practice, you can always make these changes later.

Now apply this technique to making changes in some place you really do want to change.

Technique 3: Individuals

This technique is especially useful if you want to change how you look or how you relate to others.

For practice, think of all the ways you might change yourself or another person and imagine what you or this other person might do if changed in this way. Some things you might want to change are personality traits, interests and hobbies, facial and/or physical appearance, and dress.

You can try this exercise wherever you are—wherever you see people—or you can do this by yourself either in your mind's eye or by looking in a mirror.

Now apply this technique to making changes in yourself or others you can affect.

Technique 4: Groups

This is especially useful if you want to change relationships in a work group, organizational arrangements in a company, and the like.

For practice, think of any organization or institution you would like to change if you could—ranging from a small social group, club, or society to a large institution, such as a company, school, government agency, and so on. Then think of all the changes you might make in it. Some of the things you might consider changing include: number of people, tasks, physical location (offices, space), available resources (material objects, equipment), budget, power relationships among people, mission or purpose of the organization, policies and procedures, and your role in the organization.

Don't worry about making useful changes, since you are just practicing, but if anything useful comes out of this, you can always make these changes later (or suggest them if you're not empowered to make them).

Now apply this technique to making changes.

MAKING CHANGES

Things, People, Places or Systems that Need Changing	*Changes to Make*

CHAPTER 13

EMPOWER YOUR MIND
Make Your Emotions Work *for* You

While positive emotions, such as love and joy, help us enjoy life more and feel more creative and productive, negative emotions, such as anger and fear, can also benefit us by protecting and defending us. They can warn us about things that might hurt us, or they can mobilize us to strike back at something harmful. For example, the flight or fight response triggered by danger is a survival mechanism as applicable in the corporate jungle as in the real jungle—instead of fighting a hostile lion with a powerful weapon or running away if you don't have one, you fight a corporate adversary if you can win the power struggle or remain quiet and go along if you can't.

When we lose control of our emotions, however, they can hurt us. For example, at work, if you don't control your anger or frustration, you can blow a slight into a big insult that turns into a feud. And that can not only make you feel worse, but can result in your losing a job.

Even when an uncontrolled explosion seems to achieve its immediate purpose, it can still have long-term negative effects on relationships and on personal satisfaction. By contrast, if you stay in charge of your emotions or turn anger into a diplomatic or creative way of asking for or going after what you want, you can avoid problems and achieve your goals.

∎How to Channel Uncontrolled Emotions

Gary was angry about his failure to break in as an independent publisher in the music business. For five years, he had been doing everything right and ethical. With hard work, he had signed talented songwriters and performers and had spent much time and money trying to pitch his songs to recording companies. But nothing seemed to work. Eventually, he began to feel more and more frustrated and angry. Finally, though, he felt he had found his chance—a performer who sounded so great he was sure she could create the excitement needed to break through. He put aside everything else to work on developing her career for about six months. His plan seemed to be working, when, suddenly, his star performer backed out of a booking. Gary got angry and insisted she do it—that she abide by her contract. His insistence led to a screaming fight on the phone, which ended with her saying: "Talk to my lawyer." This was followed by fights with her lawyer. The upshot was that the singer walked out, despite their contract, and since Gary had no resources to fight her and a lawyer, he couldn't do anything. His anger had provoked a confrontation that he was powerless to win.

For a moment, the expression of anger had made him feel better. He angrily insulted the singer and put her down for not living up to the contract, which might have been technically true. But the results were self-destructive. His angry explosion interfered with a key relationship that could have been a breakthrough for him. Instead, he ended up feeling the hurt victim of her actions, not realizing how much his own anger-fueled actions had turned him into that victim.

Had Gary been able to control his emotions and had he been willing to discuss some alternatives, he might not only have kept her and avoided legal problems, but eventually he might have guided her breakthrough and his own. How? By:

➤ taking some time out to calm down;

➤ using some calming self-talk;

➤ using a physical trigger to remind himself that he was getting too excited and needed to do something to calm down.

■Achieve Results with the Controlled Expression of Emotion

While the *uncontrolled* expression of an emotion, as in Gary's case, can be self-destructive, the *controlled* expression of the emotion at the right time can be just what's needed to achieve the desired effect.

So how do you do this? How do you channel and control your emotions to express them in creative ways or avoid expressing them in ways that will be destructive to yourself and others? The techniques in this chapter are designed to help you control and channel your emotions so you express them or hold them back as appropriate to the situation.

Since anger is the most destructive of the negative emotions in the work place and in everyday life, this chapter will focus on how to control and channel it and related feelings that can trigger it (such as jealousy, envy, resentment, feelings of betrayal, and the like). However, you can apply these techniques to controlling and channeling other negative emotions, too.

Recognize Your Feelings

The first step toward getting your feelings under control and channeling them is to become aware of how you feel. Then you can acknowledge these feelings and stop yourself from expressing them in an inappropriate way or at an inopportune time. It is clear that you are angry if you yell or scream, tell someone off, or otherwise demonstrate anger. But even before these outward expressions, there are inner mental or physical signs of anger, and if you are aware of them before you explode, you can short-circuit the process and then mentally decide if you want to express your anger or not. In fact, groups that try to help men overcome their violence against women use this kind of approach. They help the men become aware of the signs of their anger so they can hold themselves back and channel it away from abusing women.

Exercise 44

PICKING UP ON THE SIGNS OF ANGER

(Time: 10–15 minutes)

Get in a calm, relaxed frame of mind. Then focusing on the screen in your mind's eye, think back to times when you were angry. See the scene appear on the screen before you like a film. Then, imagine you are winding the film back to a time before the incident that provoked your anger occurred. Watch the scene unfold.

Now pay attention to how you experienced this. Be aware of the sensations in your body. Be aware of how you are holding yourself. Notice any changes in the tension of your muscles. Notice any changes in your self-talk or the thoughts going on in your mind. Notice how you are feeling when you are angry or are becoming angry.

Then let go of that image. Turn the projector off or rewind the film. Feel yourself releasing any anger. Feel any anger gone; experience that release. Then notice the differences in how you feel now and how you felt before. Be aware of the way you felt when you were angry or becoming angry compared to when you are not.

Then repeat the process to see if there are other ways you experience becoming or being angry, or repeat this to increase your awareness of the way you felt the first time. Again, focusing on the screen in your mind's eye, think back to times when you were angry. See the scene appear on the screen before you like a film playing in front of you. Then imagine you are winding the film back to a time before the incident occurred.

Now notice how you experienced this. Be aware of the sensations in your body. Be aware of how you are holding yourself. Notice any changes in the tension of your muscles. Notice any changes in the self-talk or thoughts going on in your mind. Notice how you are feeling when you are angry or becoming angry.

Then let go of that image. Turn off the projector or rewind the film. Feel yourself releasing any anger. Feel any anger gone; experience that release. Then notice the differences in how you feel now and how you felt before. Be aware of the way you felt when you were angry or were becoming angry compared to when you are not. Notice if you had the same feelings just now as you had before. Be aware of any new or different feelings you had.

Finally, keeping in mind the ways in which you experience becoming angry or feeling angry, release any feelings of anger you may now feel. You are very comfortable, very calm and peaceful now, although you are conscious of how you react when you are angry and know you may react that way in the future.

These are the signs to look for when you feel yourself becoming angry in the future. Then, keeping in mind these signs, but feeling very comfortable, calm, and peaceful, let go of what you have experienced and return to the room.

∎Six Ways to Control Your Anger

Once you feel the signs of anger coming on, you can, if you wish, stop yourself from expressing it or channel it to avoid expressing it inappropriately or destructively. Say you feel your boss is tearing you down for something that wasn't your fault. You feel ready to blow up, but rather than let your feelings out, which might lose you your job, you can hold yourself back and control just how, when, and where to express your feelings. The goal is not to be a wimp, but to manage the expression of your feelings so you express them wisely. For example, your anger at your boss might lead to a reasoned discussion of the problem, resulting in a successful outcome.

How do you deal with that anger? How do you stop it, deflect it, and channel it? Here are six effective ways to control anger.

1. *Ask for or take time out.* This is a way to get away from the situation or person who is causing you to feel angry. Time out also gives you some time to calm down, get your feelings under control, and if appropriate, check your assumptions or the information you have been given that are causing you to feel angry.

After all, you could be wrong. Time outs can be combined with one of the visualization techniques (pages 207-208) that can help you let go of and release or redirect your anger in a more positive way.

2. *Use calming self-talk.* By telling yourself calming things, you direct your attention away from what is bothering you and counter the physical feelings that are contributing to your anger. Calming self-talk can also short-circuit any immediate impulse you have to lash out verbally or physically and help you feel more detached and less emotional about the situation. You might tell yourself things like: "Calm down . . . Relax . . . This problem isn't so important. . . . You don't have to react now. . . . Don't take this personally. . . . Don't let this bother you." You can also use self-talk to guide you into the process described next—personal projection (or detachment).

3. *Use personal projection to remove yourself from the situation.* In this case, you simply imagine yourself not there. You mentally go away, or you experience yourself stepping out of yourself and watching yourself, so you are no longer emotionally affected by the situation you are in. Although you are fully aware of and in charge of the process, you become like an observer or film director, rather than an actor, in your own film. You can use self-talk to guide you into this state, or simply visualize or experience yourself somewhere else.

4. *Don't take it personally.* This is a good way to deflect a tendency to react defensively, when someone's negative or accusatory behavior is not so much due to something you have done as triggered by the person's own problems. If you can tell yourself, "It isn't me . . . He (or she) is just angry and is taking it out on me," you can help to distance yourself from the situation, so you feel less upset and angry. Then, you may find that if you just listen and don't express anger yourself, the other person will share what is really going on, and the problem will resolve itself.

5. *Let go of your anger through visualization.* While some visualizations can be done quickly (even in the midst of the situation causing you anger), others take longer and generally require some

private time. So this technique is best when you apply it to an ongoing situation or you are able to take some time out. Here are some visualizations you can use. Choose those that feel most comfortable to you, or create your own.

Exercise 45

FIVE VISUALIZATIONS FOR RELEASING ANGER

(Time: 1–2 minutes for visualizations 1, 2 and 4; 2–5 minutes for visualizations 3 and 5)

[*Visualization 1: Releasing the Anger by Grounding It out* (You can do this one on the spot.)]
As you feel the anger rising within you, visualize it coming in like a beam of negative energy from the person or situation that is upsetting you. Then, imagine this energy moving downward within you and dispersing harmlessly into the ground.

[*Visualization 2: Stopping the Anger by Blocking out the Cause* (You can do this one on the spot. It also can be combined with one of the other techniques.)]
In this technique, you simply imagine a wall of white light or a bubble or dome of protection around you. It is a barrier between you and the situation or person causing the anger. As you sit or stand behind this barrier, you can deflect everything the person says or the events that produce anger. You are safe, isolated, and protected inside.

[*Visualization 3: Releasing the Anger by Projecting It out and Eliminating It* (You may need a little time in a quiet space to do this)]
Get in a very relaxed state and imagine a large screen in front of you. Then imagine you are projecting the anger within you, like a laser beam, onto the screen. Next imagine you are holding a ray-gun and shooting at that anger. Each time you zap it, you experience the anger releasing and draining away.

[*Visualization 4: Releasing the Anger by Making the Person Causing the Anger Smaller* (You can do this one on the spot or later. It's especially suitable if the person causing the anger is more powerful than you, or if you feel this person has a strong emotional power over you.)]

In this visualization, you will release your anger by making that person seem smaller and, therefore, less powerful and less important to you. Start by seeing yourself talking to this person. See him or her doing whatever it is that makes you angry. Then, as you talk, see this person shrinking in size. Notice his or her voice becoming fainter and fainter. Meanwhile, you are feeling stronger and stronger and more powerful, while this person is becoming less and less powerful and important in your life.

Then, see yourself saying good-bye and leaving this tiny person, feeling very powerful yourself. Finally, let go of this image and return to your everyday consciousness.

[*Visualization 5: Releasing the Anger by Taking Mental Revenge* (This one is usually best done later in a quiet private space. It's a technique that works as a release for some people; others find it makes them even angrier. If you find it's a helpful catharsis for you, use it. Otherwise, if you feel your anger level going up, don't.)]

To use this technique, get into a relaxed state and then imagine yourself or a representative taking some action to appropriately punish the person who has wronged you. In the beginning, mentally ask yourself the question: "What can I do to get a just punishment or revenge for . . ." You fill in the blank with a description of what the person has done. Then, like in a film, just sit back and observe what happens. Let yourself enjoy the "film."

Afterwards, let go of the experience and return to normal consciousness. When you do, notice if you feel better now. If so, this is a good technique for you. If not, if you still feel angry or even more so, this is not a good technique for you. Try a different approach in the future.

Learn from the Experience

Although this approach is something you might do later to transform a bad experience into something that has some benefit, it can also be an anger-releasing technique. It helps release anger because the knowledge that the situation can be used later for your own benefit can help you feel better as it happens. It can help you detach and see the situation in a more neutral way, because you realize that you have the ability to transform what is negative into something positive.

To use this technique, create a reminder to yourself to help you feel better. Tell yourself something like: "I'll be able to learn from or profit from this experience later. So don't be so upset now." Or if it is possible at the time, you might think: "What can I learn from this situation that I can use in the future?" or "How can I turn this situation into something from which I can profit?" Or, later, in a quiet, private space, ask yourself these questions. Consider how the bad experience you have just had can be used to teach you something or guide you in the future; how can it be turned into a steppingstone to an opportunity from which you can gain. By reminding yourself that every experience has this positive potential and knowing that you can take some time as it happens or in the future to imagine how these possibilities might be realized, you can help release your emotional upset and anger.

CHAPTER 14

EMPOWER YOUR MIND

Break the Habits that Hold You Back

We all have habits or blocks we'd like to change. For example, some people react to a promotion or new relationship they really want by thinking: "I'm not good enough to get it." Such thinking can undermine your confidence and cause you to unconsciously sabotage your goal. In the end, your actions prove your thinking. Still other people have a negative view of the world—they expect the worst to happen and fear any change, thinking things will only get worse. This attitude helps guarantee that things will go wrong and reinforces the "See, I told you so" attitude. If these or other patterns or attitudes are holding you back, don't let them. Habits can be broken; blocks can be eliminated.

∎How Negative Thinking Creates Negative Results But Positive Change Creates Success

Since negative thinking feeds upon itself, it can be difficult to break the cycle. In fact, many people with a negative outlook feel more comfortable when an obstacle turns up, because that not only reinforces the habit, but they can use the obstacle as an excuse for not achieving their desired goal.

Sadly, many people learn to enjoy complaining as a way to gain satisfaction from all the things that go wrong. It's the "misery loves company" phenomenon—unhappy people look for someone to whom to complain, and then feel better for the support and sharing. When complaining becomes a way of life, the cycle is again difficult to break. Complainers don't realize that their attitude contributes to the many misadventures they experience. Indeed, recent research shows that a negative attitude can contribute to illness and slow down the healing process; a positive attitude contributes to wellness and healing. Our attitudes and emotions actually change the chemistry in our brain to make us function more or less effectively.[1]

But negative attitudes can be changed. We can actively intervene to break and change a cycle of negative feelings and experiences—with dramatic positive results.

That's what happened to Madeline: The youngest child, she had two older brothers who constantly criticized her, and she came to think of herself as always being wrong. By extension, she came to view everything around her that way too. If something hadn't yet gone wrong, it probably would. She looked for faults in other people and in the world generally; it helped her feel better about herself.

Because she was so judgmental, she had few friends. Because she found so many things wrong with others, she liked few people, and people, in turn, didn't like her because she was so negative and aloof. She complained of being lonely, never realizing it was she who pushed people away. At the same time, she wondered why her life seemed to go so badly. She worried about what would happen next, believing that would go wrong, too. She often nixed suggestions for the future, fearing what might happen. Thus, her negativity created blocks in her relationships and cut her off from many opportunities. But even Madeline was able to change after decades of negative thinking. You can, too.

---

[1] Bill Moyers, *Healing and the Mind,* New York: Doubleday, 1993.

∎A Changed Attitude Can Change Experience: Reprogram Yourself

If, like Madeline, you have negative attitudes and patterns that interfere with any area of your life—your relationships, your enjoyment of things, your ability to accomplish something—you can change them with positive personal reprogramming. This technique helps turn negative attitudes and patterns into positive ones. The process involves becoming aware of your negative, pessimistic thinking and then reminding yourself again and again to shift your orientation. Eventually, this new outlook becomes a new positive habit. The basic process is a simple one, though it involves repeated concentration to reinforce the desired change until it becomes automatic.

The following techniques illustrate some ways you can stop your negative thinking and turn these negatives into positives. While I've incorporated symbols and suggestions that have worked for me, what's important are the principles underlying these techniques. Feel free to adapt and change them to incorporate what feels comfortable for you.

Stop Your Negative Thinking with a Trigger

One way to eliminate negative thinking is with a trigger or cue. Each time you feel a negative emotion—such as anger, fear, dislike, or boredom—the trigger makes you aware of the feeling. Then, recognizing the feeling, you can detach yourself from it, remind yourself you are in control of your feelings, and act to make a change.

Just about anything can be a trigger—an object, a word, a physical motion. One motion that is easy to use is a special (but unnoticeable) hand gesture. To use it, simply touch your thumb to your third finger, as a reminder that you are feeling something negative and that you want to get rid of or transform that feeling. The advantage of an unobtrusive hand movement is that it is something you can do immediately (an object may not always be accessible, and a word might be blotted out by your negative thoughts). But feel free to use whatever works for you. The key is to build up an association between that physical movement, object, or word, so whenever you use it, it blocks your negative feeling and thinking.

To build this association, practice conditioning yourself to make a connection between the trigger and paying attention to a negative feeling. Here's one way to create this association.

Exercise 46

STOPPING NEGATIVE THINKING WITH A TRIGGER

(Time: 3–5 minutes)

Take a few minutes each day for about a week or two to focus on the trigger you want to use to alert you to a negative feeling. First decide on the trigger (a hand gesture, an object, or a special word).

Then take a minute to concentrate on this gesture, or object, or word. Be aware that whenever you take this action, you will focus on any negativity you are experiencing. Remind yourself that whenever you are experiencing any negativity, you will immediately pull this trigger. Then, when you pull this trigger, you will be able to remove yourself from the negative feeling you are experiencing and look at it and say to yourself: "I don't want to feel this way."

To build up the association and practice using your trigger, think of something that annoys you, makes you angry, or makes you feel negative in any way. Then, as soon as this thought comes to you, pull your trigger. Pay attention to it. Notice that your trigger stops the negative thought.

Try another negative thought or image. Again pull the trigger. Do this a few more times and tell yourself that in the future any time you experience anything negative, you will pull the trigger to make yourself aware that you are feeling something negative, and you can step outside that feeling and stop it.

Once you have built this association, whenever you feel negative about something, simply pull the trigger to make you aware of those negative feelings and stop them. Say you feel yourself getting angry in a confrontation with someone; you're about to hurl an insult or you feel like hitting the person. Simply pull your trigger instead. You'll feel a sense of detachment and will calm down. Or, if you are feeling sad and depressed, pull the trigger to step outside yourself and detach from those unhappy feelings. You'll remind yourself that those feelings are separate from you, that you can control them, and that you can do something different to make the bad feelings go away. In short, as soon as you sense negative feelings coming on, pull the trigger to stop those feelings from coming and send them away.

Clearing Out Negativity by "Cleansing" It Out

Once you realize you are experiencing negative feelings or thoughts or are around someone who is negative, you can get rid of those negative experiences with a simple cleansing technique. Initially, a physical action works best since it is more concrete and dramatic. Later, you can create a visualization of yourself cleansing out this negativity, and you can use this visualization at any time, unlike a physical gesture that might be out of place.

Exercise 47

CLEANSING OUT NEGATIVITY

(Time: 2–3 minutes)

Practice this technique for a week or two until it becomes second nature. Then repeat this exercise whenever you want to physically cleanse yourself of negative feelings.

Stand or sit up straight. Imagine you are in a shower, and, with this image in mind, run your hands over the top of your head and down your neck. Imagine, as you do, that you are cleaning off any negativity you are experiencing as you do. Feel that negativity coming out of you and into your hands. Take your hands away from your neck and shake out the negativity. Imagine it dissipating into the air and disappearing. Repeat this process a few times—move your hands from the top of your head to your neck, then shake them out in a quick, sweeping gesture. Each time you do, more and more negativity is drawn away from you and disappears into the air.

Next, take your right hand and sweep it down your left shoulder and left arm. As you do, imagine any negativity within you going into your hand and shake it out. Feel the negativity being shaken away. Now, take your left hand and sweep it down your right shoulder and right arm; shake that negativity away, too. Again, repeat this process a few times, so you feel all the negativity drawn away from these parts of your body.

Finally, using your right hand, sweep any negativity from your left side and thigh and down to your knee. Using your left hand, sweep any negativity from your right side and thigh down to your knee. Repeat these steps a few times.

When you're finished, you should feel clean and refreshed; all the negativity should be gone.

Reverse Negative Feelings

Another way to get rid of negative feelings, once you have identified them, is to turn them around by asking yourself what you can do to create the opposite, positive feeling. Suppose you feel discouraged because you failed to get a desired job or promotion; instead of feeling discouraged or put down, ask yourself what you can do to change that feeling. For example, in a relaxed state ask yourself: "What can I do to build myself up?" or "What can I do to feel a sense of accomplishment?" After asking your question, remain in this relaxed state and listen for an answer (paint a picture, fix the car, reorganize my desk) and do it—or imagine yourself doing it.

Similarly, if you have had an argument with someone and are feeling angry, you might ask something like, "What can I do to feel warm and loving again?" or "How can I turn my anger into something positive?" Listen for an answer and then do whatever you imagine yourself doing (play with your puppy, take a walk on the beach, write a poem).

In some cases, the response to your question will be something you realistically can do, and then it makes sense to do it. If you can't reasonably act on the response, however, visualize yourself doing it. The effect will be much the same, and your negative feelings will drain away, transformed by your creative positive thinking.

The following exercise will help you make this transformation. Practice the process, and later you can use it in response to any situation in which you feel negative.

Exercise 48 _____

TRANSFORMING NEGATIVES INTO POSITIVES

(Time: 3–5 minutes)

Find a quiet place where you can be alone. If you are experiencing negative feelings about anything in your life now, practice using those. Otherwise, think of a negative incident in your past.

Concentrate on the experience for a minute or two and ask yourself: "What bothers me about the experience? . . . What makes me feel so bad about what happened?" Listen to the answer. Whatever happened, identify the basic problem causing the negative feelings. Then ask yourself, "What can I do to turn the situation around?" or "What can I do to feel better?" or "How would I do things differently if I did it again?" or "What can I learn from what happened to make things better in the future?" The particular situation will determine what question to ask, or you may want to ask several questions.

Then, without trying to consciously answer the question, listen to your inner voice. It will tell you what you need to do. It may take some time to get an answer, but be patient. Just listen and wait for something to come.

If nothing comes, repeat your question or try a different one. When you get your answer, if it's something you can and want to do, do it immediately or as soon as possible. It will help you turn your negative feelings into positive ones. If the answer is something you can't or don't want to do, visualize yourself doing it.

In either case, this exercise will help you release the negative feelings you have built up around a situation and will help you create new, more positive feelings around the experience you have put in its place.

_____

■Affirming Negatives Away

Yet another way to get rid of negative thoughts and feelings is with positive affirmations—positive statements made in the present tense to assert that something is so; for example, "I'm skilled and confident and know I will reach my goal." When you use affirmations, choose those that are as exactly opposite the negative thought or feeling you are experiencing as possible. You'll find they're a quick remedy that you can use at any time, unlike visualizations, which require more time and an opportunity to be alone.

To make affirmations most effective, repeat them to yourself again and again, so they become etched in your unconscious or inner mind and become part of you. You might want to write them on cards and put them in your wallet, in a desk drawer, on a mirror, on a wall, or in some other place where you will see them regularly.

Here are some sample affirmations you can use to counter typical negative situations. You can use these or create your own to counteract something negative you have experienced.

> ➤ I feel enthusiastic, excited, and upbeat.
> ➤ I feel optimistic and certain I will get what I want.
> ➤ I know exactly what I am doing. I feel completely confident and sure about myself.
> ➤ I know I have the power to earn all the money I need.
> ➤ I have some great people and associates around me.
> ➤ I know I am doing a good job and others will recognize my contributions.
> ➤ I will get everything I need to do done in time to make the deadline.
> ➤ I like my job and find the work interesting and challenging.
> ➤ I know I am making (or have made) the right choice. I don't have to apologize for my choice to anyone or feel guilty for having made it. I am doing (have done) the right thing.

As an added bonus, you can use affirmations even when you don't feel negative, to increase your feelings of confidence, recommit yourself to a goal, strengthen your sense of personal identity, and generally feel good and upbeat.

You can use these affirmations by themselves or combine them with other techniques, such as a trigger or a cleansing technique. The advantage of either combination is that after you have acted to stop or chase away the negativity, you add something positive to fill the gap created by its absence, making the negativity less likely to return.

■Think Positive Thoughts

In summary, if you have negative experiences, feelings, or thoughts or are confronted by negative people, there's plenty you can do to eliminate those feelings and replace them with positive thoughts, feelings, and experiences. The process begins with becoming aware of when you feel negative or are being affected by negative people. Then, you can work on eliminating negative thoughts from your life by transforming them into positive thoughts, feelings, and experiences.

EMPOWER YOUR MIND
Turn Problems into Opportunities

CHAPTER 15

We all encounter problems. The difference between dealing with them successfully or unsuccessfully is summed up in one word—attitude. The key to success is a positive, constructive response. If you see your problems as challenges and stepping-stones, you can find possibilities in your problems and deal with them productively. For example, with a positive attitude, you can turn a setback at work or the loss of a job into the beginning of a new career. You can transform a conflict in a relationship into a learning experience that leads to greater understanding and intimacy. You can find ways to profit and grow from a bad experience.

In this chapter you'll find techniques that will help you respond to everyday problems creatively and productively, that will help you turn problems into opportunities for new growth and success. They will help you to:

➤ find the good in a bad situation;

> ➤ learn from your problems—discover new directions and find ways to shape your future life based on the problems you currently experience;

> ➤ profit from your problems—find ways to make money or gain other rewards tomorrow from something difficult that happens to you today (see Chapter 16).

∎Turn Lemons into Lemonade: How to Make Something Good out of a Bad Situation

The lemons-into-lemonade—negative to positive, bad into good—approach is enshrined in numerous clichés: "Make the best of a bad situation," "Every cloud has a silver lining," "It's a blessing in disguise," but the truth behind them has made these clichés endure. The essence of lemons-to-lemonade thinking is when you encounter a lemon, instead of feeling sour or bitter, find ways to use that lemon (say by adding sugar) to create something refreshing and enjoyable. With this basic approach to life, you can reshape just about any bad situation and find positive gains.

I have met many people who use the lemons-into-lemonade approach. For example, when Ted, a salesman, gets stuck in traffic, instead of getting angry and anxious as many drivers do, he uses this time to get out of his car and meet the drivers around him and tell them about his product. Usually, he meets a half-dozen new buyers for his product. When Andrew, a bachelor in his thirties, waits in line for anything, he uses this time to meet new women among those standing near him.

This lemons-into-lemonade, negative-into-positive approach is a creative, productive way to deal with a problem and turn it into a win-win situation for yourself and others. To some extent, people do this naturally when they confront obstacles and overcome them. But if you can develop this attitude into a systematic, automatic response to any negative situation, it becomes a way of life. Then, whenever a problem arises, you automatically look for ways to turn it around. You quickly put aside the feelings of frustration, anxiety, anger, or other upset responses and use the energy created by these feelings to make positive transformations.

If you're not used to looking at experiences this way, it will take some time to change your usual mode of reacting. You have to learn to stop or block your negative feelings (see Chapter 13) and break the chain of negative ideas that sometimes develops when something bad occurs.

Think of Ted again. What if, when he was stuck in traffic, he engaged in negative thinking? He might start thinking about all the appointments he was missing, the phone calls he couldn't make, the deal he might lose because he was late, and so on. As a result, he'd end up feeling tense and agitated, and there would still be nothing he could do to change the situation. The negative thoughts would have shut out positive thinking. Instead, Ted made lemonade. He used the time and made several useful contacts.

Even if you're not Ted, someone with a positive orientation in the same situation might recognize there isn't much he can do to change the situation; remind himself that when it's over, he can make the necessary calls to explain what happened; and recognize that worrying won't help. As a result, he will stay calm and relaxed and use the time to do something productive. For instance, this might be a good time to make plans for the future and jot down some notes, listen to an educational cassette on the tape deck, or brainstorm ideas for a new project.

In short, the negative-to-positive person knows to stay calm and look for positive outcomes in response to a negative situation, instead of letting the situation trigger a state of continuing upset and fretful thinking. This orientation, in turn, triggers a creative response that opens the doors to productive, positive solutions.

If you tend to react negatively to a bad situation, the first step is to stop this process. Then, with these negative thoughts pushed away, you can focus on ways to come up with positive, productive alternatives. If you already have a "what will be will be" philosophy, you can start right in on coming up with creative alternatives to negative situations.

The following exercises are designed to help you change your point of view, so you can respond positively to negative situations. Practice this technique by selecting particular situations where you want to apply this approach. As this orientation becomes automatic, you can apply it almost without thinking to virtually any situation you encounter.

∎Step 1: Put an End to Negative Associations

If you tend to get upset or angry when you encounter a problem or if you start thinking about all the negative possibilities that may result, you have to get these feelings or thoughts under control and stop them before you can allow the more positive thoughts and reactions in. One way to do this is by using the triggering or cleansing techniques described in Chapter 14 to help you become more objective and feel less negative. In addition, the following thought techniques will help you deal with the specifics of any situation.

Exercise 49

TALKING YOUR WAY OUT OF NEGATIVE THINKING

(Time: 3–5 minutes)

Talking to yourself can be effective, because you are in effect inviting your "reasonable parent" to step in to reason with your "unruly child," who has become angry and anxious in response to the situation. After your parent has gotten your child under control, your rational and responsible adult can take over to direct your thinking down more productive avenues.

To use this technique, start talking to yourself as soon as you catch yourself becoming angry or upset or as soon as you notice that you are thinking of other bad things that might happen. Recognize that this is the child part of you and invite the parent part of you to step in to counsel with that child. This parent part is very sensible and rational, very forgiving and warm, and thus, can help your child by suggesting ways to stop the negative thoughts and feelings. As these stop, you can interject positive feelings and thoughts.

To start, ask your parent to step in and talk to your child to get that child under control. Some of the things your parent might say are:

➤ "Why are you so angry and upset? There's nothing you can do about that right now, so why not relax and calm down?"

➤ "Don't think such negative thoughts. They'll only upset you."

➤ "Those bad things you are thinking are only possibilities. They may never happen. You can act to prevent them, or, if they happen, you can come up with creative, effective ways to deal with them."

➤ "Why don't you think about something more pleasant now? Your thoughts are only making you upset."

➤ "You are dwelling on the same problem and are coming up with the same thoughts again and again. You need to do some more creative, productive thinking."

➤ "There's no reason to blame yourself. It wasn't your fault. Even if it was, you can't do anything about the past now. Think of what you can do in the future to make things better."

Exercise 50

BLANKING OUT NEGATIVE THOUGHTS

(Time: 1–3 minutes)

An alternative way to stop negative thinking is to blank out all thoughts for the moment. Rather than talking to yourself, concentrate on thinking and feeling nothing.

Again, catch yourself when you feel negative emotions or are thinking negative thoughts. Then, as soon as you do, say to yourself: "Blank out," or use some other word, phrase, or image you associate with going blank, and experience your mind going blank. To help you do so, imagine yourself looking at a plain black screen—or if you prefer, it can be a soothing color, like white, light green, or blue. As you look at it, all thoughts in your mind disappear. Notice that as you look at the screen, you feel calm and relaxed. Any feelings of anger or annoyance totally fade away.

If thoughts or feelings try to creep back in, repeat the phrase "Blank out" or whatever trigger you are using to yourself. If you are alone, you can say it aloud for reinforcement. If others are present, say it to yourself.

Continue looking at the blank screen and experience this blankness for a few minutes until you have calmed down or until any negative associations running through your mind are gone. Then you are ready to fill your mind with new positive ideas.

Exercise 51 _____

FINDING REASSURANCE FROM YOUR "INNER EXPERT"

(Time 1–3 minutes)

Another approach is to imagine that an expert is seated or standing beside you or that you are talking by phone. This expert is there to soothe you.

Ask your expert for help and just listen as the expert talks to you in a reassuring voice, saying things such as:

- ➤ "Calm down. Don't worry. Things will turn out all right."
- ➤ "Just relax. Stay cool. Count to ten. Focus on your breathing."
- ➤ "You're feeling calm, relaxed. This situation doesn't bother you. It'll all work out. Just be patient and relax."

Let the expert keep talking to you for a few minutes until you feel calm. Then you're ready to move on to thinking positive ideas.

■Step 2: Brainstorm to Turn Negatives into Positives

Once you have tamed your negative feelings and feel in charge once again, you're ready to work on developing alternatives. Your goal is to think of win-win possibilities for yourself and anyone else involved. You want to come up with ways to make changes or to turn something negative into something as beneficial as possible. Then you can choose the best approach from these options.

Exercise 52 _____

BRAINSTORMING TO FIND ALTERNATIVES

(Time: 3–5 minutes)

The key to coming up with successful ideas is to let your imagination go, using the two-step brainstorming process (previously described) to come up with various possibilities. Then you can implement those that are realistic or, if necessary, propose them to the others involved.

When this technique is new to you, have a sheet of paper handy on which to write down all your ideas. Later, you can do this exercise in your mind and make a mental note of those ideas you want to use.

As usual, get in a calm, relaxed state. If necessary, use one of the exercises on pages 224-226 to help you detach or to stop any negative thinking. Then ask your question. Make it as specific as possible, and frame it in a positive, open-ended way: for example, "How many ways can I . . . " or "What are all the things I could do to benefit from this current situation?"

As you ask your questions, remind yourself that once you overcome this particular difficulty or obstacle, you may be in even better shape than when you began because you have looked at all the options and may have discovered new possibilities you hadn't considered before the difficulty arose.

∎Step 3: Evaluate the Possibilities

The final step in the lemons-to-lemonade process is to evaluate the ideas you have come up with and imagine the likely outcomes if you put a particular idea into practice. The process involves (1) going over those ideas you feel have some merit, (2) expanding them to decide if they are workable, and (3) figuring out how to implement them.

Suppose in brainstorming about a promotion you didn't get and how to handle it, you came up with the idea of taking on some free-lance work to supplement your income. The next step might be thinking about the types of free-lance work available, and, then, about how to go get that type of work. Or, say you brainstormed about how to deal with a rent increase and decided to find additional money-making uses for your house. The next step might be to determine what those things might be (for example, rent out a room or conduct a free-lance business from your home). Then you could explore each proposed solution even further (for example, how should you go about renting out a room—to whom and for what; or what kind of business might you start).

As before, it is helpful to write down your ideas. This will not only help to stimulate creative thinking, but will help you to systematically organize your ideas. As you become more adept, you can do the process mentally.

In short, the steps needed to turn a negative into a positive are

1. step away from the problem so you aren't emotionally upset by it;

2. let your imagination roam freely to come up with alternatives (reminding yourself that these alternatives might even make things better than they were before);

3. choose among these alternatives to select the one that's best for you.

■Step 4: Put Your Ideas into Action

Finally, if you have come up with an idea or several ideas you like, put them into action as soon as possible. Decide what you need to do to make the idea workable (for example, write a letter describing your plan, put an ad in the paper to find a client, go to a store to get supplies, make a list of activities for an event), and then go out and do it.

Coming up with the possibilities is just the first step in turning problems or negative experiences into positive ones. Once you have developed positive ideas, you must put them into action to make them a reality.

■Turn Disasters into Opportunities

In addition to turning around everyday problems and negative situations, the lemons-into-lemonade approach can help you turn more serious difficulties and even disasters into guides to where to go next. The first step is to acknowledge the seriousness of what happened. Then use it as a learning opportunity and perhaps you'll be able to change your current direction and focus and move on to something new.

It is important to be creative, resilient, and ready to move on when calamities occur, because in such situations it is easy to sink into depression and feel totally devastated and immobilized by the experience. In extreme cases, it may even become a permanent response, but it doesn't have to.

For example, years ago, I saw the inspiring film *The Other Side of the Mountain* about a woman who had been an up-and-coming competition skier. She trained actively, determined to be the best, but when she was on the verge of making it, she skied off the mountain and broke her spine. She was flat on her back in the hospital for months, and, at one point, near death. But with determination, she survived, and though she lived in a wheelchair thereafter and had only the slight use of one hand and arm, she became an inspiring teacher.

Like the ski accident, the results of some disasters can't be reversed, but for most of us, the results are not irreversible and we can learn how to avoid them in the future. Even if you made mistakes that brought on the calamity, accept this, forgive yourself, and work on moving on. Recognize that something terrible happened and acknowledge the part, if any, you played in contributing to it. Then stop beating yourself up. Make any amends you reasonably can and after that focus on what you can do to move on.

Remind yourself that *you* need to do this; you need to find that strength within yourself. Even though you may need and should accept help from others, you need to stay in charge to make decisions. It's important to work out your own solution after a very difficult situation to strengthen yourself. Once you do, you can find the seeds of a tremendous opportunity in what was once a disaster. As Napoleon Hill says in his books about success, look within the adversity you have experienced for the seed of a personal benefit. Look for what you can learn about yourself and what to do next. Use the experience to help guide you to where to go next. Ask yourself how the experience can help you make decisions and grow into whatever you do next.

Five Steps to Turning Disaster into Opportunity

There are steps you can take to turn a disaster or difficult problem into an opportunity or source for learning and for finding new directions.

1. *Recognize the disaster.* You need to truly believe it is time to shift gears—that the situation you are in can't continue; you have to pull the plug and find a new outlet. Sometimes it can be hard to let go, especially when a situation has been building up for some time—the problem drags on; you keep hoping that things will change . . . you keep hanging on or do a little bit more. But at a certain point, you have to let go; you have to walk away and separate yourself from the situation. You have to acknowledge that nothing will change unless *you* make that change.

When should you do this? Take a little quiet time to ask yourself that question and listen to what your inner voice tells you to do now. Keep waiting and hang on? Do a little more to turn things around? Or cut your losses and move on now? Ask yourself what is *really* best for you, not what you wish were true. Use the exercise on pages 230-231 to help guide you.

2. *Separate yourself from the experience.* Pull yourself away from what happened; imagine you are standing apart from it, looking at it from a distance, as if it weren't happening to you. Look at it in a detached, objective way; let go of self-destructive emotions, such as blaming or punishing yourself for what happened. If you caused or contributed to what happened, simply recognize this fact and let go of any blame or shame. View yourself as someone who was learning and who may have made some mistakes along the way, but now you are a different person. You have grown and are wiser now, due, in part, to what happened.

An added benefit of separating and detaching yourself is that you can reduce, eliminate, or control the intense emotions that focus your attention on what occurred and free yourself to learn from what happened and move on.

The following exercise will help you gain this detachment if you are still caught up in such emotions.

Exercise 53 _____

SEPARATING YOURSELF FROM A DIFFICULT EXPERIENCE

(Time: 5–10 minutes)

Find a quiet place where you can be alone and comfortable. Close your eyes and relax. Concentrate on your breathing for a minute or two.

Now imagine that there is a stage or movie set before you and visualize the experience that is upsetting you as if it were occurring on this stage or set. See yourself as simply another character in the drama. At the same time, you are in the audience, watching it unfold.

As you watch, notice the characters moving about on the set. Everything is life-size as you experience it. As you continue to watch, notice that the stage set seems to be moving away from you. It is also getting smaller. As it becomes more distant, it is shrinking.

As you observe this happening, you feel freer. With your eyes still closed, lift your hands and rub them across your head and neck. Now shake out your hands, as if you were cleansing yourself of any bad feelings that may be lingering. Then run your hands down the sides of your arms and your body. Again shake them out, so any negative feelings are shaken away. Run your hands along your stomach, waist, and legs. As you do, even more negative feelings are sucked out and shaken away.

Finally, look at the stage set far in the distance. It is extremely small now, about the size of a small shoe box. You or someone backstage can now pick up that whole set. Pick it up and put it in a large black trash bag. Then put a rubber band or clip around the top and throw it away.

See it land in an open pit with a fire. The flames leap up, lick the sides of the bag, and in moments the bag with your bad experience is surrounded by flames. As it burns, you feel any remaining ties with the experience slipping away. Soon, any feelings of connection are completely gone and you are free.

Continue experiencing this image and the feelings of freedom for a few minutes. Then, when you are ready, open your eyes. You'll feel detached and free of the bad experience. You'll be ready to learn from it and go on.

---

3. *Learn from the experience.* Once you feel some detachment, look critically at what happened to understand what went wrong and how you can gain from this understanding. Again, don't cast blame on yourself for the past; rather examine the incident to gain insights so it doesn't happen again.

While this examination involves a critical assessment, approach it in an intuitive, not a logical or analytical way, to tap your deep personal insights about what you have learned. Later, you can assess the value of the different things you learned and determine how to apply them.

The following exercise, based on the two-step intuitive brainstorming process will help you do this. Copy the chart on page 233 to record your insights and ratings.

Exercise 54

GAINING INSIGHT FROM THE EXPERIENCE

(Time 5–10 minutes)

As usual, get calm and relaxed in a quiet place. You should feel separate and apart from what happened. If not, use the exercise on pages 230-231 to detach yourself before beginning this exercise.

To begin, you will ask yourself a series of questions; then meditate on each one for a minute or two and write down whatever comes to mind. Don't try to think of the answers or force them; just let them bubble up from deep inside you and know that they express your inner desires and truth. (You can use the chart on the following page as a guide.)

Now ask yourself any of the following questions (choose those you feel are relevant to your situation) or come up with questions of your own.

➤ "What went wrong and why did it happen?"

➤ "What lessons can I learn from the experience?"

➤ "What kinds of mistakes were made that shouldn't have been made; how can they be corrected in the future?"

➤ "What kinds of skills or knowledge did I gain from the experience?"

➤ "What did I learn that I might be able to use in the future?"

Don't try to answer these questions consciously. Just let your unconscious mind go and let it give you the answers. Write down whatever it says. Remember, the idea is not to control the process, but to let the answers well up from deep inside you, so you get your direction from your inner mind.

When the answers stop coming, end the process. Review your answers. How valuable were they? Rate them on a scale from 0 to 5.

Keep these valuable insights in mind when you go on to the next stage of this process—deciding on your next step.

GAINING INSIGHT FROM THE EXPERIENCE

Questions	Rating (Scale 0-5)
1. What went wrong and why did it happen?	
2. What lessons can I learn from the experience?	
3. What kinds of mistakes were made that shouldn't have been made; how can they be corrected in the future?	
4. What kinds of skills did I gain from the experience?	
5. What did I learn that I might be able to use in the future?	

4. *Determine your next step.* Using the insights you have gained from the experience, apply them so you can move on successfully to something new (a new career, relationship, place). To discover the next step, begin by questioning your inner self. Then be open to the possibilities for change and welcome the opportunity for transformation. Remind yourself that it is to your advantage to take what happened and rebuild, based on the new knowledge and insights you have gained from the experience.

The following exercise is designed to help you connect with this inner knowing. You can use the chart on page 236 for writing down your insights about what to do next:

Exercise 55

DETERMINING WHAT TO DO

(Time: 5–10 minutes)

To begin, have a sheet of paper and pencil in front of you. As usual, get into a calm relaxed state in a quiet place. Again, you will ask yourself a series of questions and meditate on each one for a minute or two. Don't try to think of these answers or force them; just let them bubble up from deep inside you and know that they express your inner desires and truth. (You can use the chart on page 236 as a guide.)

Now ask yourself any of the following questions (choose those you feel are relevant to your situation) or come up with questions of your own. Write down the answers as they come:

➤ "In light of what I have learned from this experience, what should I do now?"

➤ "Should I work on rebuilding or improving what I have done in the past, or should I go on to other things?"

➤ "If I should rebuild or improve, how should I go about doing this? What do I need to do now?"

➤ "If I should go on to other things, what should I do next?"

➤ "What kind of (career, work, relationship) do I want now?"

➤ "What resources do I need to move forward?"

➤ "Whom can I turn to for help?"

As the answers appear in your mind, write them down. Take about a minute or two to meditate on each question. Don't try to answer these questions consciously. Just let your unconscious mind go and let it speak to you. Write down whatever it says. Then, when the answers stop coming, end the process.

Now review your answers and rate them. Which ones do you want to act on now? Which do you want to wait to implement? Use a rating scale of 0 to 5. Implement those with the highest rating first. Afterwards, you can put your ideas into practice.

---

5. *Pat yourself on the back.* Now that you have separated from your past experience, have learned from it, and know where you are going, take a few minutes to feel good about yourself and your new commitment to the future. Tell yourself you have made the right decision and are ready to move on. This reaffirmation will help you feel complete and confident in your decision.

Exercise 56

REAFFIRMING YOUR DECISION

(Time: 2–5 minutes)

Get relaxed and close your eyes. Now project yourself into the future—3 months, 6 months, 1 year, 3 years, 5 years—however long you think it will take to reach your goal. See yourself having achieved your goal and enjoying the fruits of your victory.

If you want a nice car or house, see yourself enjoying these. If you want to travel, imagine yourself on your dream trip. If you want a successful career, imagine yourself in that role in the future. Take a few minutes now to experience whatever it is as vividly as possible. Look around, listen, touch whatever is around you, and fully enjoy the experience.

As you see these images of success in your life, pat yourself on the shoulder and compliment yourself. Tell yourself: "Good work. You're doing great. You've really done it."

Then, after a few minutes, feeling complete, let these images go and return to the present and into the room. As you open your eyes, you will feel really good.

DETERMINING WHAT TO DO

Questions	Rating (Scale 0-5)
1. In light of what I have learned from this experience, what should I do now?	
2. Should I work on rebuilding or improving what I have done in the past, or should I go on to other things?	
a. If I should rebuild, how should I go about doing this? What do I need to do now?	
b. If I should go on to other things, what should I do next?	
3. What kind of (career, work, relationship) do I want now?	
4. What resources do I need to move forward?	
5. Whom can I turn to for help?	

CHAPTER 16

EMPOWER YOUR MIND

Turn Your Problems and Passions into Profits

*M*any things—good and bad—can be turned into opportunities for profit if only you pay attention to the possibilities and consider them in two ways:

1. From the perspective of other people's needs and desires: What do people like or need that no one is currently providing?

2. From the perspective of your own needs and desires: What do you really like to do and how can you make a profit doing it? Or, can you turn a problem you have experienced or are experiencing into something profitable?

Keep these two perspectives in mind as you go through life; they'll help you find ways to profit from your everyday experiences. Take, for example, Mrs. Fields' cookies, which were started when a woman who loved to bake cookies found that neighbors and friends loved them. She began selling them locally, then created a company, and eventually franchised it nationally. Indeed, many products have come from either people's passions or their problems. Consider the various gourmet foods on supermarket shelves devised by people who like to cook and have turned their recipes into commercial products and the various diet foods that have come from other dieting agonies.

On the other hand, a number of national nonprofit organizations were started by people who, having experienced problems or tragedies, turned their experiences into organizations that helped others. They thereby gained a sense of meaning or mission from what happened. Others have turned their difficult experiences into books that have helped other people learn from or be inspired by their experiences.

∎Turn Your Problems into Rewards

In short, there are many ways to turn either your passions or your problems into a financial profit and other rewards, if you're creative and have something of the spirit of the entrepreneur, inventor, or artist ready to break new ground. To see if you can do so, begin by asking yourself these questions:

1. *Is your problem common to many other people?* If so, there may be a how-to book, tape, workshop, or support organization you might develop that could help others deal with or resolve the problem. Even if you are not a writer, speaker, organizer, or manager yourself, could you find others with the skills you need who are willing to participate?

2. *If you have learned to deal successfully with a problem, can you help others deal with it?* If so, you might become a consultant or start a company or organization to help others in similar situations.

3. *Does the problem suggest a new product or service?* Many inventions and services get started this way. For example, one man I know designs products in response to accidents. After an accident, the company calls him in; he goes over the reasons for the accident and then comes up with devices to help avoid the accident in the future. Consider your own problems and their

product possibilities. The situation doesn't have to be as serious as an accident. Perhaps if you've had trouble locating something you want or need, if it's not on the market, others might want it, too. You might be able to develop it into a marketable product.

4. *Does the problem suggest a new type of work? As a result of your problem, have you developed new skills you can use?* A problem you experience may be a source of ideas. These ideas may be the direct result of your experience in solving the problem—you have gained new skills, have developed a new product or idea for a service, or have become so knowledgeable that you can consult on the topic.

In other cases, you may not have personally experienced or solved the particular problem, but by looking at a problem in a creative way or by coming up with ideas on how others might solve a problem, you might be able to benefit yourself and others.

The following exercise combines brainstorming with meditation to come up with possibilities and alternatives.

Exercise 57 _____

FINDING PROFIT IN YOUR PROBLEM

(Time: 10–20 minutes)

Part 1: Coming Up with Alternatives

Copy the chart on page 241 and have a pencil handy. Then get relaxed and clearly define what the problem is. Ask yourself the following questions or create questions of your own.

➤ In what ways might I be able to make a profit from my problem?

➤ What have I learned from this problem that might enable me to be an expert or consultant?

➤ What kinds of new products or services does this problem suggest? What needs does this problem suggest people might have?

➤ What kinds of new skills have I gained from this problem that I might apply in a new job or new career?

➤ Are there any other ways I might profit from my experience?

Part 2: Selecting Alternatives

Now go over the list of ideas you have generated by brainstorming. Rate them from 0 to 3. Select the top one or two ideas to develop further. Later, you can go back and select additional alternatives.

Part 3: Visualizing the Results

Again, have a sheet of paper and a pencil handy so you can take notes. Or, if you prefer, use a tape recorder to record your ideas. Then, as usual, get calm and relaxed and close your eyes.

Now imagine one of the alternatives you have selected before you on a screen. For example, if you think the problem suggests a product, see the product there; if the problem might lead to a consulting career, pursuing a new line of work, or starting a new business, project an image of whatever you will be doing on the screen.

Then focus on that possibility and ask yourself some questions about what might happen if you pursue that alternative and how you might develop it further. For example, if you are considering a product idea, imagine how that product might look and what it might do. If you are exploring the possibility of a new business or new job, think about what that business or job might be like and see yourself at work.

Then, as one question or idea suggests another, go with that. The idea is to let your intuitive mind go and think of how you might put the alternative you are considering into practice.

As ideas come to you that seem useful, write them down or tape them. If you wish, write or state your thoughts in brief outline form. Later, when you resume normal consciousness, fill in the outline; and do it soon, before you forget.

∎Turn Your Passions into Profit

Just as your problems, particularly when shared by many others, may be a source of profit, so, too, may your passions. The first step is to determine what you really love to do or would love to do, if you could do anything you wanted to do.

HOW CAN I PROFIT FROM MY PROBLEM?

My problem is:_____

Questions	Rating (Scale 0-3)
1. In what ways might I be able to make a profit from my problem?	
2. What have I learned from this problem that might enable me to be an expert or consultant?	
3. What kinds of new products or services does this problem suggest? What needs does this problem suggest people might have?	
4. What kinds of new skills have I gained from this problem that I might apply in a new job or new line of work?	
5. Are there any other ways I might profit from my experience?	

You may already know what you really want to do. If so, you can skip the next exercise, but if you aren't sure whether you have a really strong passion and commitment, use the following exercise to help you measure it. Then, if you truly have this desire, the last exercise will help you think of ways to create profitable opportunities from it.

Exercise 58

RATING THE POWER OF YOUR PASSION

(Time: 5–7 minutes)

This technique is designed to help you determine the strength of your passions.

As usual, get comfortable and relaxed. Close your eyes. Then imagine that you are in a meadow and are taking a journey along a path to a pool of water that always tells the truth. See yourself walking along this path now. The day is sunny and warm and you feel very comfortable. Now you are walking through a grove of trees, and ahead of you in the clearing, you see the pool of water.

It is glistening in the sunlight, and you go toward it. Then, standing in front of the pool, you look in. The water is very blue and clear; it is like a clear mirror.

Looking directly into this water, ask your question: "What do I really love to do?" And see the image of this activity appear on the screen. See yourself doing it and experience the joy of it.

Then, see that first image fade, and ask: "Is there anything I really love to do even more? If I could do anything I wanted to do, what would I most love to do?" Then see this image appear. It may be the same thing, or it may be something different. Whatever it is, see yourself doing this, and experience the joy of it.

Then see this image fade, and now, looking into the pool of water, ask the question: "Do I really want to turn what I love to do into something profitable? Do I really have the desire and commitment to work on doing this?"

Look in the pool for your answer. It may be a clear "Yes" or a "No," or the message or image may be less certain, a "Maybe," "Not sure,"

"Later," or a "Yes but," telling you there are other things you must do first. Allow whatever appears in the pool to emerge, as you just observe.

Finally, after you have your answer, let the image fade and turn from the pool back to the path. Now see yourself walking along this path back to the meadow. Once you are back in the meadow, you are ready to return. Count backwards from five and return to the room and open your eyes.

If the exercise has given you a strong feeling for what you want to do and a strong "yes" to go turn it into something profitable, think about how you can do this. If you have gotten a "no" or an uncertain message, don't pursue it for profit now. Consider pursuing it as a hobby or recreation, so you can continue to enjoy it. Later your attitude may change or you might decide to leave it as is.

Exercise 59

PROFITING FROM YOUR PASSIONS

(Time: 5–20 minutes)

The approach here is similar to that used in thinking about how to profit from your problems, but now you are thinking about the ways in which your passions can appeal to other people's desires or needs.

Part 1: Coming Up With Alternatives

Begin by copying the chart on page 245 and have a pencil handy so you can write down ideas. Then get relaxed as usual and after you ask each question, come up with as many ideas as you can.

Before you begin, make sure you are clear about what your passion is and that you are committed to turning your passion into a source of profit. Then ask the following questions or create others. Write down your answers.

➤ In what ways can my passion serve a real need or desire that others may have?

➤ In what ways can this passion be turned into new products or services I might offer?

➤ What kinds of skills have I gained or can I gain from doing what I love to do?

➤ What kind of business can I create or what kind of job might I look for that will let me do what I love to do?

➤ Are there any other ways I might turn what I love to do into a source of profit?

Part 2: Selecting Alternatives

Now go over the list of ideas you have generated. Rate them from 0 to 3. Select the top one or two ideas to develop further. Later, you can go back and select additional alternatives.

Part 3: Visualizing the Results

Again, have a sheet of paper and a pencil or, if you prefer, a tape recorder handy. Then, as usual, get calm and relaxed and close your eyes.

Now imagine one of the alternatives you have selected before you on a screen. For example, if you have thought about turning your passion into a new business, see yourself engaging in this business. If you think your passion suggests a service you can perform, see yourself engaging in this service. Whatever it is, project an image of what you will be doing on the screen.

Then focus on that possibility and ask yourself some questions about what might happen if you pursue that alternative and how you might develop it further. For example, if you are thinking about a new business, ask yourself what type of business it will be. If you are considering a product or service idea, imagine how that product or service might look and what you might do to promote it. If you are exploring the possibility of a new job, think about what that job might be like and see yourself at work.

As one question or idea suggests another, go with that. The idea is to let your intuitive mind go and think of how you might put the alternative you are considering into practice. As ideas come to you that seem useful, write them down or tape them so you won't forget.

HOW TO PROFIT FROM MY PASSION

My passion is:_____

Questions	Rating (Scale 0-3)
1. In what ways can my passion serve a real need or desire that others have?	
2. In what ways can this passion be turned into new products or services I might offer?	
3. What kinds of skills have I gained or can I gain from doing what I love to do that I can turn into a source of profit?	
4. What kind of business can I create or what kind of job might I look for that will let me do what I love to do?	
5. Are there any other ways I might turn what I love to do into a source of profit?	

CHAPTER 17

EMPOWER YOUR MIND

Get the Most from All Your Relationships

*T*apping into your inner creative powers can lead to better relationships with others. Not only will your first impressions be more accurate, but you'll be better able to respond to and determine whom to trust when you first meet people. In addition, your inner creative powers can help you become more sensitive to others and how they think and feel, which, in turn, will help you relate, communicate, and resolve any conflicts that might arise.

■Understanding the Other Person's Personality Style

One way to get a better understanding of someone you meet or have a relationship with is to recognize his or her personality style, much as you might assess your own personality traits. (See Chapter 8.) To recap briefly, the four preferences or orientations can be categorized as:

1. Extroversion versus Introversion
2. Sensing versus Intuition
3. Thinking versus Feeling
4. Judging versus Perception.

These can be combined broadly into four types:

1. Introverted Sensing Types
2. Introverted Intuitive Types
3. Extroverted Sensing Types
4. Extroverted Intuitive Types

Keeping these different preferences and types in mind, you can do an exercise similar to the one you did to understand your own qualities. Though you can't change another person the way you did yourself, you can shape your own actions to better respond to the person's qualities based on what you sense about this person. The following exercise will help you recognize someone's personality and suggest how you might use this information to better respond to the person in a particular situation.

Exercise 60 _____

RECOGNIZING PERSONALITY TYPE AND IMPROVING
THE RELATIONSHIP

(Time: 10–20 minutes)

The first part of this exercise is designed to help you think about someone's primary personality characteristics and how they might affect your relationship. The next part of this exercise will help you think about how to change the way you respond to this person to improve the relationship.

Part 1: Recognizing Someone's Personality Type

To begin, have a sheet of paper and a pencil handy. Then get relaxed and close your eyes. Focus on your breathing going in and out, in and out for a minute or two until you feel very relaxed and calm.

Begin by seeing an image of the person whose personality you want to understand on the mental screen in front of you. See the person as clearly as possible and put him or her in the setting in which you are usually together.

Then, just above the person's head, notice the two words—Extroversion and Introversion, which represent the way the person focuses his or her attention. Notice which word flashes more brightly or what images come to you most strongly. If the person tends to be extroverted, you will see images of people socializing and talking. If he or she is more introverted, you will see images suggesting ideas, thoughts, and reflection. And if the person is a little of both, you will see both images, though the one that is more influential will be bigger or brighter. Next, see this person expressing this characteristic. The scene can be either one you have experienced or one you imagine.

Next, just above the person's head, notice the two words—Sensing and Intuition, which represent the way he or she acquires information. Notice which word flashes more brightly or what images come to you most strongly. If he or she is primarily a sensing person, you will see images of objects and things. If he or she is an intuitive person, you will see more abstract images or impressions, representing concepts or ideas. If he or she is a little of both, you will see both images, though the one that is more influential will be bigger or brighter. Next, see this person expressing this characteristic. The scene can be either one you have experienced or one you imagine.

Now, just above this person's head, notice the two words—Thinking and Feeling, representing the way he or she makes decisions. Notice which one flashes more brightly or what images come to you most strongly. If he or she is primarily a thinking person, you will see the images of a person who tends to make decisions by thinking things through, such as a scientist, professor, or a manager studying data. If he or she is a feeling intuitive person, you will see images of someone impulsive or someone who responds from the heart—a counselor, nurse, or very caring teacher. And if he or she is a little of both, you will see both images, though the one that is more influential will be bigger or brighter. Next, see this person expressing this characteristic. The scene can be either one you have experienced or one you imagine.

Finally, just above the person's head, notice the two words—Judging and Perceiving, representing the person's orientation toward the outside world. Notice which word flashes more brightly or what images come to you most strongly. If he or she is a judgmental person, you will see the image of someone who likes structure and organization, such as someone in a very neat and organized room. If he or she is a perceiving person, you will see images of someone with a more flexible, spontaneous approach toward life and the room will be less organized, maybe even messy and chaotic. And if the person is a little of both, you will see both images, though the one that is more influential will be bigger or brighter. Next, see this person expressing this characteristic. The scene can be either one you have experienced or one you imagine.

Now, if you wish, write down what you have noticed about the person and star the person's predominant characteristics. Or you may go immediately to the next part of this exercise and make your notes later.

Part 2: Determining How to Relate Based on Personality Type

Knowing what you do about this person, imagine yourself with the person in a real-life situation. See that scene on the screen in your mind. Notice how the person is acting and think about how those actions reflect any of the person's personality traits.

Based on how you are interacting, have there been or might there be any strains in the relationship? If so, notice how the person's personality traits come into play. For example, if this person tends to be a judging person who likes order, he or she might be annoyed if things are less than orderly or imprecise. If this person tends to be a perceiving person who likes things kept loose and spontaneous, maybe he or she is resisting order and structure. Whatever the case, notice any points of tension that may have occurred or might occur in the future.

Based on what you have observed about this person or any points of tension you have noticed, think about your own actions. How do you tend to respond to this person? Is there anything you have done that has contributed to the tensions between you? Is there anything you might change in the way you act with this person that might contribute to a better relationship? Ask yourself a series of questions like these about the relationship and any changes you might make and see what answers come up. If you want to focus on a particular situation, you can do so now.

Finally, when you feel ready, let go of the images and come back into the room. If you wish, write down your thoughts and suggestions about what to do or what to change.

∎Resolving Conflicts through Visualization

Your power of visualization can help you to resolve conflicts by first conceptualizing different strategies and then deciding which one would be most effective. It's helpful to understand the five different conflict styles and when to use them before deciding which one to employ.

How Judy Resolved an Office Conflict with Creative Visualization

Judy, who worked in a sales office, was having problems with a co-worker, Teri. It began when a few humorous comments were misunderstood and escalated quickly. Eventually, Judy suspected that Teri might be talking about her behind her back and even sabotaging her meetings and phone calls. Things had gotten out of hand, and Judy felt she had to do something before they got even worse. But what? She only suspected Teri might be doing things, she didn't know for sure. Should she confront her? Say nothing? Speak to her boss, who seemed to like Teri very much, about her suspicions?

Judy took some time to visualize several possible responses she might make and the possible results of each. An angry accusation would lead only to more bitter words and more concealed sabotage. Saying nothing left things as they were with behind-the-scenes attacks. Speaking to the boss put Judy on the hot seat and might lead her boss to question her abilities. Finding ways to document Teri's actions only seemed to promise a continued conflict.

Finally, Judy imagined what might happen if she had a long talk with Teri in which she spoke about how they had once had a good relationship and discussed what had happened. Was there any way they could get back to that and put aside whatever was going on between them now? In her imagination, Teri proved receptive and the two of them worked out their problems together. Later, when she approached Teri, that's what happened. Teri realized that Judy probably knew what she was doing behind her back. But since Judy approached her not to blame or accuse her but to work out a creative solution that would be good for both of them, Teri was willing to listen. The result was that the conflict ceased, and, eventually, the two even found ways to help each other.

Similarly, if you imagine various scenarios and outcomes, based on the situation—what you know about the other person's personality type and your own personal style—you can choose among them to select the best alternative. Here's how.[1] (I'll first describe the conflict model I use and then show how you can use the imaginative process to determine what to do about a conflict you are experiencing.)

∎The Five Styles of Conflict Resolution

The five ways to respond to a conflict situation are:

1. *competing*—being forceful;
2. *accommodating*—giving in to what the other person wants;
3. *avoiding*—backing away from the situation;
4. *collaborating*—working with the other party to find a comprehensive resolution;
5. *compromising*—each person gives a little.

The best choice in a particular situation depends on a variety of factors, such as: personal and other style preferences, the nature of the situation, the importance of the issue to each party, the relationship between the parties, the power balance between them, and the costs and benefits of the proposed solutions relative to the reasons for the conflict.

These styles are based on how you respond to satisfy your own concerns and the other person's concerns. To satisfy your own concerns, you can be assertive or unassertive; and to satisfy

---

[1] This technique draws on a basic model for conflict resolution that I have been working with for some time. I initially described the model in *Resolving Conflict*, New Harbinger, 1990. This technique takes the basic concepts in this model and combines them with the use of mental imagery and self-projection into the future.

the other's concerns, you can be cooperative or uncooperative. When one is assertive to get one's own way without regard for the other person's interests, this is the *competing* style; when one is both unassertive and uncooperative, this is the *avoiding* style; when one is both self-assertive and cooperative, this is the *collaborating* style; and when one is unassertive and cooperative, this is the *accommodating* style. Finally, the *compromising* style represents the middle ground in which each party gives a little to get a little.[2]

Choosing the Right Conflict Style for the Situation

All these styles can work successfully at different times and when used by different people. It depends on the situation and what you feel comfortable with. There is no right style. They all have appropriate uses. However, there are times when one style may be more useful than others; I will list these briefly.

Use the competing style when

➤ the issue is important and you have a big stake in outcome;

➤ you have the power and authority to get what you want;

➤ you have no other options or nothing to lose;

➤ a quick decision is needed or there is an emergency;

➤ you are at an impasse and can't get group agreement;

➤ an unpopular decision is needed and you have the power to make it.

Example: You are the chair of a group that has been bickering about what action to take; the group is divided; and you have to announce your decision on the issue to meet a deadline. You announce that since the group has to do something and no one can agree, you have decided to take a certain action because you feel it is the best thing to do under the circumstances.

---

2 These five styles have been described and used extensively in educational and business management programs based on a system called The Thomas-Kilmann Conflict Mode Instrument developed by Kenneth W. Thomas and Ralph H. Kilmann in 1972.

Use the accommodating style when

➤ the issue is unimportant and you don't care about the outcome;

➤ you have little power and no or little chance of winning;

➤ the issue and outcome are more important to others;

➤ you want to keep peace and harmony;

➤ a good relationship is more important to you than the issue;

➤ you are wrong and the other person is right;

➤ others might learn from making the decision even though they are wrong.

Example: A co-worker is collecting contributions to a charity that your boss and most people at work support. You don't want to contribute, since you don't like this particular cause and would prefer to contribute to something else. However, the amount requested is small—only a few dollars—and you feel it important that your boss and co-workers see you as one of the team, so you go ahead and contribute and keep your objections to yourself.

Use the avoiding style when

➤ the issue is unimportant and you have little stake in outcome;

➤ you lack the power to resolve the situation well or at all;

➤ you can't win or have little chance of winning;

➤ you need time and want to delay until you can get information or help;

➤ you want tensions to cool down;

➤ the conflict could worsen if it becomes open;

➤ others can or will resolve the matter better.

Example: A co-worker has been pressuring you to participate in an outside activity that you don't think you want to get involved in. You aren't sure if this activity will be as interesting or as profitable as she claims and you aren't sure you have the time for it. You don't want to offend your co-worker even though she is being pushy, since you have to work together. So you put off making any decision until you can get more information and feel under less pressure to make a decision.

Use the collaborating style when

> ➤ the issue is important to both parties;
> ➤ both parties have similar power or are willing to put aside any power differences;
> ➤ both parties have a close, continuing, interdependent relationship;
> ➤ both parties are willing to spend time and effort;
> ➤ both parties are able to discuss the situation and listen to each other.

Example: You and a co-worker have been assigned to a six-month project. You have different personality styles and different ideas about how to get the project done. These differences have grown and are interfering with the project and are affecting office morale generally. If the problem isn't resolved, one or both of you could be fired or reassigned to something with less responsibility, but if you can make it work, it will be to the advantage of both of you. So you suggest that the two of you sit down and work out a way to work together. You then spend some time understanding why you clash and how each of you can change your behaviors to avoid future problems.

Use the compromising style when

> ➤ both parties have different goals and these goals are not too important;
> ➤ both parties have similar power;
> ➤ you want a resolution quickly or a temporary resolution will do;
> ➤ the resolution, though not ideal, provides short-term gain;
> ➤ collaboration or competition doesn't work;
> ➤ this resolution is better than no resolution.

Example: You have been trying to work out an agreement on the price of something you want to sell. You don't have another buyer and you want to close the deal as quickly as possible. The prospective buyer is trying to get you to offer a lower price than you normally would accept and is threatening to go to a competitor. You are angry, but need the sale; therefore to achieve a resolution, you offer to split your difference.

Recognizing Your Own Style

If you think about these five styles and how you have responded to conflict situations over the years, you will see that you usually respond to conflict in certain ways. This is your primary style. You may also have a secondary style, the next most common approach you use. Some people tend to be bimodal or trimodal; they shift between two or three usual styles.

You can discover your own style using an intuitive approach.[3] This approach can also help you to discover which style you prefer using and which styles you have the most and least success using.

∎The Scott E-R-I Model of Conflict Resolution

I call the basic conflict resolution model I use the "E-R-I" Model. The "E" represents emotions, the "R" represents reason, and the "I" represents intuition. To successfully resolve a conflict, you must work with all of these three elements.

Emotions—How to Control Them

The emotions play a disruptive role in a conflict, since they are normally the negative emotions—anger, hostility, jealousy, and envy—that make each party to the conflict upset. As a result, they interfere with understanding the reasons for the conflict, communicating successfully, choosing an appropriate approach

---

[3] There is also a written test with questions you can use to discover your own style called the Thomas-Kilmann Conflict Mode Instrument.

for resolving the conflict, and coming up with alternate possibilities that might lead to a solution. The key is thus to get rid of negative emotions and control or channel the emotions you can't eliminate. (Some techniques for dealing with the emotions were previously described in Chapter 13.) Before using a visualization technique to consider different approaches and results, you must first control your emotions.

Reason—Your Key to Understanding

With your emotions at bay, you can then use reason to consider what created the conflict and recognize the possible strategies you might choose among to resolve the problem. Conflicts arise out of different interests or values, poor communication, a lack of information, incorrect assumptions, problems with power, control, and responsibility, and difficulty in dealing with difficult people or personality clashes.

Take a little time before you use the intuitive approach to reflect on what factors are operating in your case. Ask yourself:

1. Do this person and I have different interests and values? If so, what are they?

2. Do we communicate poorly? In what way? When does this occur?

3. Is a lack of information on either of our parts contributing to this conflict? If so, how can I obtain this additional information? How can I help this other person obtain it?

4. Could I be making any wrong assumptions that are contributing to this conflict? Could the other person be making incorrect assumptions? If so, how can I check my assumptions to learn if they are correct? How can I learn what is correct? How can I help the other person to do so? Is there any way I can provide information to correct the wrong assumptions this person may have about me?

5. Are there problems of power or control that might be contributing to our conflict? Is there a battle for power? Unequal power? Do I feel as if this person is wrongly trying to control me? Might he or she feel this about me?

6. Are there problems of responsibility that might be contributing to this conflict? Am I accepting the responsibility I should? Might the other person feel I am not accepting enough responsibility or trying to take too much? Is the person accepting the responsibility I feel he or she should accept? Or is he or she accepting none, too little or too much, in my opinion?

7. Is there a basic personality clash between us that is contributing to this conflict? What is the source of this clash? Is there any way to defuse this situation? Are there changes I can make in my personality when I am around this person that might help? Is there any way I can be more accepting of the other person's personality?

After you go through this checklist and have a general sense of the types of problems that exist and types of things you might do to respond to them, you can use this background information to help inform your visualization of what to do in a conflict situation.

Use the chart on pages 259-260 to guide you through this list.

Intuition—The Path to Conflict Resolution

Once you have your emotions under control and have used your reason to understand what is happening, and are aware of the different conflict styles and when to use them, you can now use your intuition to help you choose the style that is most appropriate to a particular situation. A way to do this is by taking a mental journey in which you visualize the conflict and try applying different conflict-resolution approaches to see which one works best. (If you prefer, you can see these approaches and outcomes on a screen and imagine that you are the director of the action. Use whichever approach works best for you. The following exercise illustrates the mental journey. You can substitute the imagery of the director and the screen.)

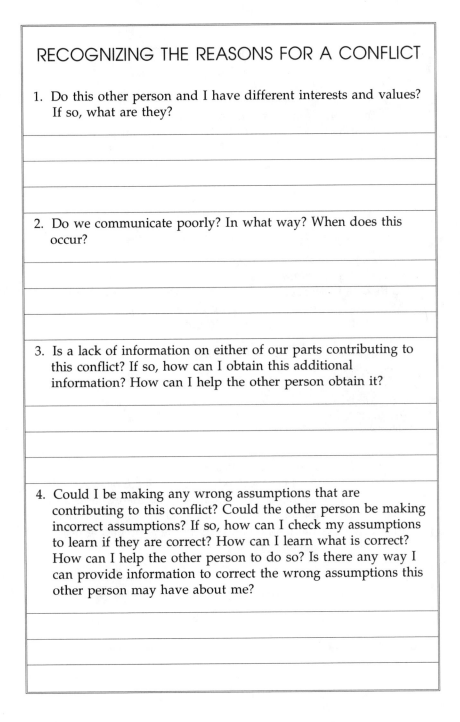

RECOGNIZING THE REASONS FOR A CONFLICT

1. Do this other person and I have different interests and values? If so, what are they?

2. Do we communicate poorly? In what way? When does this occur?

3. Is a lack of information on either of our parts contributing to this conflict? If so, how can I obtain this additional information? How can I help the other person obtain it?

4. Could I be making any wrong assumptions that are contributing to this conflict? Could the other person be making incorrect assumptions? If so, how can I check my assumptions to learn if they are correct? How can I learn what is correct? How can I help the other person to do so? Is there any way I can provide information to correct the wrong assumptions this other person may have about me?

RECOGNIZING THE REASONS FOR A CONFLICT
(continued)

5. Are there problems of power or control that might be
   contributing to our conflict? Is there a battle for power?
   Unequal power? Do I feel as if this other person is wrongly
   trying to control me? Might he or she feel this about me?

6. Are there problems of responsibility that might be contributing
   to this conflict? Am I accepting the responsibility I should?
   Might the other person feel I am not accepting enough
   responsibility or trying to take too much? Is the person
   accepting the responsibility I feel he or she should? Or is he or
   she accepting too little or too much, in my opinion?

7. Is there a basic personality clash between us that is
   contributing to this conflict? What is the source of this clash? Is
   there any way to defuse this situation? Are there changes I can
   make in my personality when I am around this person that
   might help? Is there any way I can be more accepting of the
   other person's personality?

Exercise 61

USING THE MENTAL-JOURNEY TECHNIQUE TO RESOLVE CONFLICT

(Time: 10–15 minutes)

On this journey, you will see the conflict situation, imagine different approaches and results, choose among these approaches to decide what to do, see the problem resolved, and feel good that you have resolved the problem.

Start by getting comfortable and relaxed; close your eyes. Concentrate for a few moments on your breathing going in and out, in and out, in and out. You are feeling more and more comfortable, more and more relaxed.

Now imagine yourself in a meadow. It's a warm, beautiful day, and you are standing under a tree, looking around feeling very comfortable, very peaceful. In the distance, you notice a path winding through the woods, and you follow it. It leads across a hill and to a large pond.

Now, as you gaze into the pond, you see it is very still and clear, so you can see a clear reflection in it.

As you look in front of you, you see a picture of the conflict you are involved in gradually emerge. As you watch, you see that scene played out in front of you. Even if you are in the scene you are also an observer, watching it.

As you observe, imagine that you are trying to resolve the conflict using a competing style. See yourself being forceful in trying to get your way; notice what happens and how you feel.

Now imagine you are using the accommodating style. See yourself giving in to the other person; notice what happens and how you feel.

Now try using the avoiding style. See yourself walking away from the problem. Again, notice what occurs and how you feel.

Now try using the collaborating approach. This time, see yourself spending time really discussing the problem, finding out what the other person wants and explaining what you want. Once more, notice what occurs and how you feel.

Finally, try using the compromising approach, in which you give a little and the other person gives a little. Again, notice what happens and how you feel.

Now, knowing you can choose any one of these styles and use it, reflect on the various choices you made. See the different scenes and results flash quickly before you. Notice which one seemed to work best. Which one seemed to have the best result? Which result did you feel best about?

Then choose that approach and take a few moments to see that scene play before you. See yourself using that approach and see the conflict being resolved. See the successful outcome and feel really good.

Now, when you feel ready, let go of the image and watch it fade away. Then turn away and start heading back down the path to the meadow. You can see the meadow ahead of you and there is the tree where you started. As you stand again under the tree, count backward from 5 to 1, and as you do, you will return to your room.

CHAPTER 18

ORCHESTRATE YOUR THINKING

Make Everyday Experiences Exciting and Productive

*E*veryday experiences tend to be routine and therefore uninteresting. As a result, we become impatient or bored and may find ourselves slipping into automatic pilot as we do common tasks, such as shopping, taking buses, or driving our car. Sometimes this nonthinking or unorchestrated daydreaming state can be very relaxing and even interesting.

However, if you consciously take advantage of this time to orchestrate your thinking, you can make both routine and non-routine everyday activities, more interesting. By applying empowered-mind techniques to these times you can add novelty and excitement to whatever you are doing, and, as an extra benefit, you might discover ways to enhance your skills and develop profitable ideas.

This chapter just hints at the possibilities for making your everyday experiences more interesting, productive and enjoyable. You can develop your own exercises as well.

▋Enhance the Ordinary with Mind Play

Do you feel restless or bored while you are doing something routine, such as waiting in line, being left on "hold" for several minutes, sitting at the airport waiting for a flight? Do you feel impatient or annoyed because you are stuck in traffic or in an airline holding pattern? If so, you can take advantage of such moments to engage in various forms of mind play. Mind play will not only relax you and help to eliminate negative feelings, but it can be interesting, amusing, and even profitable.

It's something I do frequently. If I find myself in one of those situations, I ask myself what can I do with this time to make things more interesting. Then I start thinking about whatever comes up, using a quick prioritizing and selection process to decide what to focus on. One long plane trip triggered ideas that led to a children's book. Stuck in freeway traffic, I have focused my imagination on ideas for games and song lyrics that were later saleable.

The basic mind play process starts with:

1. being aware that you are feeling impatient, bored, annoyed, or that your mind has gone blank;

2. consciously telling yourself that you want to take this time to use your mind creatively or productively;

3. quickly coming up with possibilities on which to concentrate;

4. selecting among these possibilities;

5. focusing on using your intuitive mind to come up with ideas or to be more receptive to what is around you.

Exercise 62

SIX EMPOWERED-MIND TECHNIQUES
THAT ADD ZEST TO YOUR LIFE

There are many techniques you can use to add richness and enjoyment to your life; I've described six that work well. You can also create your own.

Technique 1: Active listening

With your eyes closed or open (as you prefer), concentrate on listening to what's going on around you. Notice any sounds you are making. Notice the sounds in the room or nearby; also be aware of any sounds further away. Now imagine that you are creating a spatial map of the different sounds you hear. Notice where the different sounds with different tones and intensities might fall on the map. Experiment by focusing on different sounds—one at a time, two or more together, shifting your attention from one sound to another. Intervene in the listening process; for example, imagine the sound changing or moving closer or further away. Try combining the sounds you hear with your other senses; for example, notice what images or stories different sounds suggest or notice where you hear different sounds on your body.

You'll find you can actively shape how you hear the sounds around you and increase your ability to experience sound by how you listen.

Technique 2: See the world differently

Imagine you are looking at the world through a camera, each scene a picture with a frame around it. Then look closely at what you see, as if it were a snapshot or photograph in an album. Pay attention to the color, shape, composition, and feeling of the picture. Notice details, patterns, the people in the scene. Make changes in the image you see (not just those changes that might actually occur). For example, increase or decrease the size of the frame. Zoom in and out. Rearrange things in the picture or change the way they look; imagine a scene with a river running through it or with a mountain moved from the right to the left side of the picture. Or focus very intently on a small section of a scene and see how much you can see that you might otherwise not pay attention to. For example, really look at a flower—start with the overall image and gradually zero in on smaller and smaller areas, such as the petals, the color, the veins in the flower.

After a while, you'll discover that you become more and more perceptive as you slow down and *really* look.

Technique 3: Sense more

Another way to add interest to everyday experiences is to remind yourself to pay more attention to your senses so you more fully experience the texture and feelings of everyday things. Some ways to pay more attention include:

Part 1: Touch. Focus on what you perceive with your sense of touch. Notice how things feel more intense when you touch them, not only with your hands, but with other parts of your body—your arms, feet, legs, shoulders. Notice the differences you perceive when you are touching something or someone or experience something or someone touching you. Some things to pay attention to when you focus on your touch include:

➤ textures (smooth-rough)

➤ temperature (warm-cold)

➤ pressure (soft-hard)

➤ resistance (yielding-resistant)

➤ activity level (passive-active)

Note your preferences and reactions: What textures, temperatures, pressures, resistances, level of activity, and so forth, do you prefer and how do you react to the different types of touch? As you touch or are touched by different things or on different parts of your body, compare the way you feel.

If possible, try closing your eyes, so you can focus even more; then move your hands onto another part of your body, doing the touching slowly. Pay attention to the various qualities you feel (such as shape, size, texture, roughness, angularity, and so on).

Part 2: Feelings. Focus on what you perceive through your emotions; notice how you feel around different things or in different places. Some responses to notice are:

➤ good to bad

➤ positive to negative

➤ calm to energized

➤ friendly to hostile

➤ curious to bored

➤ happy to sad

Close your eyes, so you can be even more focused on your emotions. How does your body express these different feelings? Notice such things as your heartbeat, the strength of your pulse, the tension or sense of relaxation in your muscles, and your breathing.

Part 3: Smell. Focus on what you perceive through your sense of smell; notice the different smells around you. Notice the differences in what you smell in different settings. For example, notice contrasts such as:

➤ acrid-sweet

➤ pleasant-unpleasant

➤ strong-weak

What images or associations come to you as you encounter different smells? Try to find words to describe what you are experiencing. We don't have as many words in our vocabulary associated with smell as we do for our other senses, since smell is generally less important to us than our other senses and is less developed. But often smell acts subliminally to make us feel more positive or negative about something (just think of all the perfumes, deodorants, air fresheners, and the like which are on the market to make us feel better).

Again, close your eyes, so you can be even more focused on what you smell. Notice how these different smells surround you and notice how they come from different directions and how they range in intensity. Imagine yourself in a bubble of smells; then notice how you can sense smells of different intensities in different places within this bubble.

Part 4: Touch, emotions, and smell. After experimenting with each of these senses individually, try putting them together in varying combinations.

As you pay attention to two or more senses at a time, notice what you experience. For example, combine touch and feeling, touch and smell, feeling and smell, or combine all three. Perhaps combine one or more of these senses with hearing and close your eyes so you can be more focused on these less dominant senses.

Technique 4: Imagine yourself in different scenes/ different roles

Imagine yourself in different settings—either as yourself or as someone else.

For example, when you are at a restaurant, you might imagine that you are the chef in the kitchen or the waiter moving from table to table.

Or visualize yourself as that beautiful woman with the heavy gold jewelry or that hip-looking man who reminds you of a movie star. As you imagine you are this other person, imagine you are acting as this person or seeing the room from this person's point of view.

Or project yourself into different settings. Say you are a tourist at an exotic location—don't just look, project yourself into the scene. You can even imagine what the scene might have been like decades or centuries ago when it was peopled very differently. You can do this at an art gallery, museum, shop—anyplace that stimulates your imagination. Whatever the situation, after you project yourself into the scene, use the other sensing techniques to enhance the experience.

Technique 5: Become an active spectator

Another way to enrich your everyday experiences is to become more actively involved in them. In effect, you become a participant even though you are only observing or listening to something. For example, at a concert, sports event, or theatrical performance, you can use the various techniques just described to create a more intense, moving experience. (As an added bonus, when you do participate, you can step up your level of involvement, using these techniques.) Here are some additional brief exercises you can do to become a more active spectator:

1. As you listen to music, create a scene in your mind by concentrating on seeing images, experiencing smells, and letting the music trigger associations.

2. Experience the music in different parts of your body; visualize it traveling throughout your body and notice how it feels.

3. As you dance, imagine yourself in different roles, pay attention to the way the music feels against your body as you move, or invite the music to suggest images and associations. Imagine you are in a different place. Imagine you have become different colors, objects, plants or animals, or people. Notice how these changes alter how you move and how you experience the movement or music.

4. As you exercise (run, lift weights, do aerobics), use these mind-expanding exercises to feel and experience more. Direct your attention to your body by focusing on your breathing or on your muscles as you move. Pay more attention to what's around you.

Close your eyes and notice the sounds, smells, and feelings you have as you shift your attention around the room.

Technique 6: Take a mental journey

Mental journeys add interest and excitement to whatever you are doing. You can't do this exercise in the middle of an important project or when doing something that requires your full concentration, such as driving a car, but if you have some time—relaxing on the beach, waiting for a plane—or when you have a few minutes at home or at work, it makes a great break.

You can readily create your own scenarios for where you want to go and then go, or you can use a guided trip (see Chapter 11).

Here are a few scenarios; develop one if it appeals to you, or start with your own themes:

➤ a journey into outer space

➤ a trip backward or forward in time to a selected location

➤ a journey underwater

➤ a trip to another country

➤ a hike through a wilderness area

➤ be a kid in a toy store

And so on—the possibilities are endless. Just ask yourself where you want to go and start your trip.

▮Gain Insight from Everyday Experiences

When things go wrong, it's a little like getting an error message on a computer—it tells you something isn't quite right and suggests some things you can do to fix the error.

Picking up the Clues

Typically, you have to interpret the feedback or signals you get to decide what to do next. It's rare that feedback will shout at you—"Do this!"—but as you think about an event, a sense of what you should do will come to you, and, if you feel on an intuitive, gut level that your interpretation is correct, go for it.

By looking on an experience—even a bad one—as a signal or opportunity from which to learn, not just a problem to be overcome, you can use the event as an opportunity to make changes and move on to other things.

To pick up on the signals you receive:

1. *Look for significant events.* An event is significant or worthy of attention when it is

➤ especially disruptive of your routine;

➤ unusually surprising or unexpected;

➤ especially distressing or disturbing;

➤ highly emotional (positive or negative).

In essence, these events are experiences that stand out in some way. We obviously can't pay attention to everything that goes wrong, but when an event stands out above the rest, that's the time to take a special look to see what clues it suggests for what to do or what to change.

Often the events are themselves harbingers of change, since they involve a shake-up or a potential transformation that invites or requires a response. But at other times, an event can seem inconsequential and might easily be ignored. Therefore, in paying attention to everyday events, look not only for unusual or unexpected occurrences, but also take into account more subtle events that just don't feel right. Listen to your inner voice and teach it to pay attention. It is your internal warning signal.

2. *Reflect on what happened.* Ask yourself questions, such as:

➤ Is this event telling me to do something differently or to change something?

➤ What can I learn from this event about myself and about what I want?

➤ Does what happened suggest what I should do next?

Open yourself up to the answers that come; don't try to shape them. Essentially, you are talking to your unconscious and asking it to respond. Use the relaxation and visualization techniques described earlier to help you get in the relaxed frame of mind necessary to tap into this inner part of yourself.

3. *Listen to the answers.* You may want to write down both the questions you want to ask and the answers you get.

4. *Review the answers.* Do you feel strongly that they are telling you what you should do now?

5. *If your answer is a strong feeling that you should act now—if it really feels right—start taking steps to put that idea into action.* If you're not sure, monitor the situation for a while and review it later to see if the signal has gotten stronger.

The following exercises will help you develop your ability to pay attention to events, interpret them, and use them when making decisions about the future.

Exercise 63 _____

REMINDING YOURSELF TO PAY ATTENTION TO THE CLUES

(Time: 1–2 minutes)

One good way to stay attuned to events is to remind yourself to pay attention at the beginning of each day. After a while, you will do this automatically and there will be no need for these reminders. But initially, by practicing this technique, the reminder will help you to stay alert.

Soon after you wake up while you're still in bed or while you're standing in front of your bathroom mirror, take a minute or two to say to yourself something like

"I will stay alert and pay attention to the events that happen in my life. I'll take special note of those that seem especially difficult, unusual, or that otherwise stand out."

Exercise 64 _____

RECORDING EVENTS

(Time: 1–2 minutes)

To keep track of events that stand out, keep a notebook with you and jot down a line or two as a reminder. Later, when you have time, think about the significance of that event and how to interpret or gain insights from it. For example, your notes for the day might read something like

➤ ". . . Conflict with boss over new project."

➤ ". . . Debate with friend over legality of a new business project he is involved in."

Alternatively, take a minute or two at the end of each day to review the day's events. Notice if any event or events stand out. Write down whatever comes.

_____

Exercise 65 _____

EXAMINING EVENTS FOR INSIGHTS

(Time: 3–5 minutes)

After you have noted any events that stand out, take some time at the end of the day to review them. This is the time to decide if any of the events are significant enough to look into for insights. To do this, go down your list of events and quickly rate them as follows:

A—key event; something to look at right now
B—possibly significant event; something to look at more closely if I have time
C—fairly ordinary, routine event; something to ignore

Then, if you have any As, look at those events more closely. Don't be concerned if you don't have any because these are, by definition, outstanding and unique. Look next at the Bs if you have any. If you feel any are important enough, look at them more closely. Should you have only Cs, ignore them; these events are ordinary and routine.

_____

Exercise 66

MAKING CHOICES BASED ON A SIGNIFICANT EVENT

(Time: 3–5 minutes)

Once you have selected an event you feel is significant, the final step is using brainstorming and visualization to decide how to use that event to tell you what to do.

Find a quiet place and focus on the event. Review what happened in your mind's eye. Then, ask yourself a few questions about the event, such as:

"What does this event mean to me?"

"Why does it seem so significant?"

"What is it telling me about what I should do next?"

Listen to the answers and write them down. Let any ideas come into your mind; don't question or analyze anything. When the ideas stop coming, evaluate them more critically and choose those that make sense to you.

After you practice this technique for a while, you'll find that insights from the events that stand out in your life will come automatically. When they do, you can automatically go from an awareness of the event to obtaining insights from it to making decisions based on it. You won't need to write anything down. But until you find yourself responding automatically, it's helpful to begin by reminding yourself to pay attention, write down what you observe, choose the events that seem significant, and write down what you might do as a result of that event.

Follow Your Intuition

Besides looking for signs and opportunities in events, a related approach lets you "go with and learn from the flow."

I have met many people who have used this approach effectively. Beyond a certain point, instead of fighting the flow of events, they accede to the power of these events and use them as a source of information to provide a direction for the future. Then they use that information to go on.

▪Incorporate Empowered-Mind Techniques into Your Life

As you work with the empowered-mind techniques, you'll find they will become second nature. And that's the goal—to make this approach to thinking, feeling, and responding to whatever happens so automatic that it becomes part of you. Then you no longer need the formal techniques because you'll be able to work with this approach, at will, for any purpose whatsoever. You'll also be able to create your own techniques to apply to specific situations.

In fact, I want to encourage you to do this. Draw on your own creative resources to adapt these processes, using your own images, symbols, and ways of imagining and thinking things. As I noted in the introduction, I have included here techniques that have worked for me and for people in various workshops I have conducted. But there is nothing sacrosanct about particular words, phrases, images, or methods.

What works is the overall approach, which is based on receptively gaining insights, deciding how best to react to them, and actively responding, using creative visualization, brainstorming, and other techniques to tap into, mobilize, and expand these intuitive powers. The more you use these methods to activate your inner mind, the more you will find they trigger your own creative processes.

I want to encourage that. The goal is to make the empowered-mind approach, which is facilitated by these techniques, your way of approaching life.

Index